Liberating the Corporate Soul

Building a Visionary Organization

Richard Barrett

compliments of the

**Executive
Development
Center**

More than simply a majestic vision, Richard Barrett's book brilliantly describes the ways and means for business leaders to create the compassionate and viable future we urgently need on our beautiful planet.
—**Godric E.S. Bader**, F.R.S.A., Life President, Scott Bader Commonwealth Ltd.

If every corporate executive bought this book and assigned it for in-house management development courses, the world would become a better place.
—**Hazel Henderson**, author, *Building a Win-Win World* and *Creating Alternative Futures*

As we approach the new Millennium the world seeks clear thinkers with visionary concepts to help unravel the challenges before us. Richard Barrett's inspiring new book *Liberating the Corporate Soul* weaves a rich tapestry balancing heart and soul with a practical down-to-earth corporate vision for the future.
—**Craig** and **Patricia Neal**, Co-Founders, Heartland Institute

Liberating the Corporate Soul presents a convincing rationale for making ethical and socially responsible behavior the best foundation for building and maintaining a high performance, globally successful business.
—**Robert W. MacGregor**, President, Minnesota Center for Corporate Responsibility

Liberating the Corporate Soul gives a powerful set of tools for organizational transformation. I highly recommend it.
—**Ann Svendsen**, Consultant and author of The Stakeholder Strategy: Profiting from Collaborative Business Relationships

Practical advice to tap the source of creativity and innovation which every business seeks.
—**Ron Nahser**, President and CEO of The Nahser Agency/Advertising, Chicago

The bold, practical blueprint we need for moving business to the next evolutionary level. Sweeping, brilliant, a sense of the grandeur of the new paradigm of business.
—**Martin Rutte**, President Livelihood, co-author *Chicken Soup for the Soul at Work*

Liberating the Corporate Soul is a must read for leaders who want to shape a government built on values, innovation, and greater efficiency.
—**Jody Zall Kusek**, Director of Strategic Planning and Performance Manage-ment, U.S. Department of the Interior

Liberating the Corporate Soul achieves the impossible: it integrates the intangibles of ethics, vision, and consciousness into a tangible measure-ment system.
—**Marcello Palazzi**, Bsc, Msc, MBA, Co-Founder and Chair, Progressio Foundation, The Netherlands

Liberating the Corporate Soul provides a paradigm shifting look at how business leaders can harness the creative potential of their staff and their organizations. The author concisely develops and explains several tools that will enable managers to create an organizational foundation that will foster alignment, accountability and strategic focus.
—**Tad McKeon**, MBA, CPA, CQM, 1997 Senior Examiner, Malcolm Baldrige National Quality Award, co-author, *Transforming Home Care: Quality, Cost and Data Management*

This book has captured the true challenge of business today: nurturing values-based organizations to which employees and other stakeholders commit. It is also an excellent guide to achieving this goal which is proving to be the most important success factor of our times.
—**Margareta Barchan**, CEO and President, CELEMI, Sweden

This book breaks new ground in helping business leaders take responsibility for the whole. It encourages us to build a better world through business.
—**George E. McCown**, Co-Founder and Managing Partner, McCown, De Leeuw & Co., Chairman, World Business Academy

If you want to install in your company a climate of trust, harmony, creativity and vision . . . If you accept to be honest about your own values and ethics . . . Jump on this book, it is one of the best I know, linking a new vision with concrete and effective tools helping you to revitalize and reenchant your enterprise.
—**Marc Luyckx**, Forward Studies Unit European Commission, Brussels

Liberating the Corporate Soul

Liberating the Corporate Soul

Building a Visionary Organization

RICHARD BARRETT

Boston   Oxford   Johannesburg   Melbourne   New Delhi   Singapore

Recognizing the importance of preserving what has been written, Butterworth-Heinemann prints its books on acid-free paper whenever possible.

 Butterworth-Heinemann supports the efforts of American Forests and the Global ReLeaf program in its campaign for the betterment of trees, forests, and our environment.

Library of Congress Cataloging-in-Publication Data
Barrett, Richard, 1945–
    Liberating the corporate soul : building a visionary organization / by Richard Barrett.
        p.   c.m.
    Includes bibliographical references (p.   ) and index.
    ISBN 0–7506–7071–1 (alk. paper)
    1. Social responsibility of business.   2. Industries—Social aspects.   3. Business ethics.   I. Title.
HD60.B38   1998
658.4'08—dc21   98–29208
                                                                          CIP

British Library Cataloguing-in-Publication Data
A catalogue record for this book is available from the British Library.

The publisher offers special discounts on bulk orders of this book. For information, please contact:
Manager of Special Sales
Butterworth-Heinemann
225 Wildwood Avenue
Woburn, MA 01801-2041
Tel: 781-904-2500
Fax: 781-904-2620
For information on all Butterworth-Heinemann publications available, contact our World Wide Web home page at:
http://www.bh.com

10 9 8 7 6 5 4

Printed in the United States of America

To those who have the courage to bring their whole selves to work.

Epigraph

Business has become the most powerful institution on the planet. The dominant institution in any society needs to take responsibility for the whole. But business has not had such a tradition. This is a new role, not well understood or accepted. Built on the concept of capitalism and free enterprise from the beginning was the assumption that the actions of many units of individual enterprise, responding to market forces and guided by the "invisible hand" of Adam Smith, would somehow add up to desirable outcomes. But in the last decade of the twentieth century, it has become clear that the "invisible hand" is faltering. It depended on a consensus of overarching meanings and values that is no longer present. So business has to adopt a tradition it has never had throughout the entire history of capitalism: to share responsibility for the whole. Every decision that is made, every action that is taken, must be viewed in light of that responsibility.

—WILLIS HARMAN, COFOUNDER OF THE WORLD BUSINESS ACADEMY

Table of Contents

Foreword

The human race is in the midst of making an evolutionary leap. Whether or not we succeed in that leap is your personal responsibility.

—SCOTT PECK

This is not a book for the faint-hearted or those who lack the courage to live in alignment with their deepest motivations. It is a book for those who know there is a better way to do business. A way that encourages every employee to become all they can become. A way that allows people to bring their deepest values to work and have them celebrated. A way that welcomes diversity as a pathway to innovation. A way that puts reengineering into a transformational framework, refocusing it as a tool for health maintenance rather than radical surgery. A way that seeks to create symbiotic alliances with customers, suppliers, the local community, and society at large and a way that supports the evolution of the planet and the human race.

Many of those who have openly declared their allegiance to these new principles of business have been the subject of scathing media reports when they have not been able to live up to their espoused values. These pioneers should be thanked not ridiculed. To fall short of living by a higher set of standards is not an occasion for rebuke, but an occasion for learning. All those who care about the future of our children and the future of the planet owe these pioneers our heartfelt gratitude. They have demonstrated that it is possible to change the philosophy of business and be financially successful. This book is dedicated to these people and all those that have the courage to explore three of the most exciting new frontiers of business—employee fulfillment, social responsibility, and compassionate capitalism.

THE BOOK

Whenever I embark on writing a book, I am never quite sure where it will lead me. It is like starting a journey with only a general idea of where the destination lies and the vaguest of notions of how to get there. Trusting in the outcome is an important part of the journey. This book has been such a journey. I started out with two ideas. The first idea was that organizational transformation must look and feel a lot like personal transformation. The second idea was that the values held by successful companies must be similar to the values held by successful individuals. These two ideas led me on a journey of discovery that gladdened my heart. I not only found these two theses to be correct but also found underneath the tough rhetoric of Wall Street a small but growing number of successful businesses that live by values that are concordant with the highest moral and ethical principles. This book celebrates their success and provides a road map and tools for those who want to travel the same path.

The book begins by exploring what I believe are the two most critical issues for business in the twenty-first century—values-based leadership and employee creativity. Chapter 1 highlights the importance of corporate culture in addressing these issues. It examines the implications of the shift in metaphor from the organization as a machine to the organization as a living entity. The chapter closes by identifying the six characteristics of long-lasting successful companies.

Chapter 2 focuses on values and the changing role of the organization in society. It highlights the impact of current business philosophy on environmental degradation and social disintegration. It shows why the current philosophy is unsustainable; why there is hope for the future; and how the values shift that is beginning to take root in business is good for employees, good for the environment, good for society, and good for the organization.

Chapter 3 highlights the role that corporate culture plays in employee productivity, creativity, and innovation. It details the physical, emotional, mental, and spiritual needs of employees and the nine motivations that must be satisfied to bring about employee fulfillment. It focuses on the importance of employee participation and the need to develop mechanisms to institutionalize innovation. In the twenty-first century, the most successful organizations will be those that align the personal missions of their employees with the mission of the organization.

Chapter 4 consolidates the four human needs and nine personal motivations into Seven Levels of Human Consciousness. The Seven Levels of Human Consciousness are translated in turn into Seven Levels of Employee Consciousness and Seven Levels of Corporate Consciousness.

Chapter 5 shows how the model of the Seven Levels of Corporate Consciousness has been used to create a series of Corporate Transformation Tools to help organizations build values-driven corporate cultures. The use of one of the tools—the Values Audit Instrument—is illustrated using case studies. The application of the Values Audit Instrument to identifying cultural integration issues in mergers and takeovers is also discussed.

Chapter 6 explores the concept of the values-driven organization in greater depth. A new model for creating inspiring vision, mission, and values statements is described with reference to a case study. The use of the model in building linkages between the personal motivations of employees and the vision and mission of the organization is described.

Chapter 7 shows how an organization can create a values-driven strategic planning framework by linking the organization's vision, mission, and values to a Balanced Needs Scorecard. The six-part scorecard helps organizations focus on their physical, emotional, mental, and spiritual needs by measuring the organization's performance in terms of corporate survival, corporate fitness, corporate evolution, customer and supplier collaboration, corporate culture, and the organization's contribution to the local community and society.

Chapter 8 describes four of the most important cultural characteristics of high performance organizations. Each of the characteristics—trust, meaning, community, and ownership—is discussed in detail. The importance of shared values, personal mission, creating boundaryless organizational structures, and teaching employees to think like owners is emphasized.

Chapter 9 describes the Seven Levels of Leadership Consciousness and the differences between managers and leaders. It also defines the leadership values that will be necessary in the twenty-first century to build values-driven organizational cultures.

Chapter 10 describes the use of the Leadership Values Assessment Instrument for supporting senior executives in developing their leadership skills. Three case studies are presented and a three-stage leadership development program is described.

Chapter 11 draws together the models and tools described in earlier chapters into a values driven process for building a visionary organization.

Chapter 12 provides a summary of the seven principles that are driving the new theories of business.

ACKNOWLEDGMENTS

I am very grateful to all those people who over the past three years have helped me shape and mold my ideas into their present form. I would particularly like to thank Martin Rutte and Oscar Motomura for their deep friendship and support; Ismail Serageldin, Vice-President for Environmentally Sustainable Development at the World Bank, who encouraged me to explore the boundaries between spiritual values and sustainable development; Mary Jane Bullen, who gave me her unconditional support while I was Values Coordinator at the World Bank. Craig and Patricia Neal of the Heartland Institute in Minneapolis and numerous other conference organizers, who gave me a platform on which to expose my ideas in the major cities of North America and Europe; my partner, Joan Shafer for her challenging commentary and detailed editing; and finally my wife, Nancy, and son, Chris, who continue to give me their undying support wherever my mission takes me.

1

Introduction

I am often asked, "How do you explain Nucor's success?" My stock reply is that 70 percent of it has do with culture and 30 percent has to do with technology. Without a doubt, Nucor's culture is its most important source of competitive advantage, and it always will be.

—KENNETH F. IVERSON, CHAIRMAN, NUCOR CORP.

We're going to see companies increasingly assume that what they stand for in an enduring sense is more important than what they sell.

—JIM COLLINS, COAUTHOR, BUILT TO LAST

If you were to ask a group of enlightened CEOs to tell you the two most critical issues for business in the next century they would answer, "How to tap the deepest levels of creativity and the highest levels of productivity of our employees." In a world where competition has become global and where knowledge and technology flow readily across international boundaries, companies are learning that the only way to build real competitive advantage is through their human capital. This is forcing companies to take a hard look at their corporate cultures and values. Enlightened leaders are learning that employee fulfillment, environmental stewardship, and social responsibility will be the keys to increased productivity and creativity in the future. The values that corporations hold are increasingly affecting their ability to hire the best people and sell their products.

This increasing emphasis on values is due to two causes—a global shift in the underlying assumptions that govern our society; and a growing awareness of the causal link between the rapidly escalating worldwide environmental and social issues and the philosophy of business. Civic leaders, community representatives, and environmental groups are demanding that businesses stop polluting the air, water, and land. At the same time, they are asking companies to take a more socially responsible attitude toward downsizing and factory closure or relocation. Growing numbers of investors are refusing to buy stocks in companies that behave irresponsibly. Growing numbers of customers are choosing products that are manufactured by socially responsible companies. And, growing numbers of employees are expressing a preference to build careers in companies that have values-based cultures where they can find meaning and make a difference through their work.

Who you are and what you stand for are becoming just as important as what you sell. The values that corporations hold are increasingly affecting their ability to hire the best people and sell their products. Governments and communities are recognizing that corporate self-interest is leading to the destruction of the planet's life support systems and the social fabric of society. The era of corporate autocracy is coming to an end. There is too much at stake for it to be otherwise. In the words of Robert Haas, CEO of Levi Strauss, "In the next century, a company will stand or fall on its values."

VALUES-BASED LEADERSHIP

The world is searching for a new type of corporate leadership—one that is able to operationalize the win-win opportunities inherent in a corporate culture that supports social responsibility, environmental stewardship, and employee fulfillment. Companies are discovering that, far from being a burden, attention to these three areas is becoming a key ingredient in their recipe for success. Enlightened leaders are finding a dynamic balance between the interest of the corporation, the interest of the workers, the interest of the local community, and the interest of society. They are recognizing that the only way to increase the levels of productivity and innovation necessary to survive and prosper in the twenty-first century will be to transform their corporate values radically.

Corporate transformation begins with a shift in the values and behaviors of the leadership. Corporations don't transform. People do. Corporate transformation is fundamentally about personal transformation. It will happen only if there is a willingness on the part of the leader and all those in authority to live according to values that are less focused on self-interest and more focused on the common good. For transformation to be successful, the espoused values and behaviors must become pervasive throughout the organization. Only when the leadership walks the talk and the espoused values and behaviors are fully integrated into the human resource systems will the culture change cascade down through the organization.

Enlightened leaders know that to attain long-lasting success they must build a values-driven corporate culture that is independent of their identity. When a leader retires or moves on, the culture must continue. When an organization has a successful culture, it promotes a new CEO from within.[1] When a company is not successful, the task of creating a successful culture is usually given to an outsider or an internal candidate with an outsider mentality. In *Corporate Culture and Performance*, John Kotter and James Heskett of the Harvard Business School describe the career paths of 11 leaders who have successfully led major culture changes in large organizations. They state that all these leaders brought with them an "outsider" perspective—"that broader view and greater emotional detachment that is so uncharacteristic of people that have been thoroughly acculturated in an organization."[2]

For a company to find long-term success it must become a living independent entity that reflects the collective values of all employees. The task of the leader is to give birth to this entity—to give the company its own sense of purpose and vision—to liberate the corporate soul.

The company itself must become the ultimate creation.[3] It must have its own identity separate from that of the leader. The strength of the identity will be directly proportional to the degree to which the organizational culture embraces the common good. The fundamental challenge facing business leaders is to create a corporate culture that supports and encourages all employees to tap into their deepest levels of productivity and creativity by finding personal fulfillment through their work. When people find meaning in their work, they naturally tap into their deepest levels of creativity and highest levels of productivity. The dichotomy between work and play disappears. This will occur only if employees share a common vision and values. People are clamoring to work for organizations that care for them as a whole person and allow them to bring their highest values to work.

BEYOND REENGINEERING

Establishing a values-driven organizational culture goes beyond reengineering. Michael Hammer, one of the originators of the concept of reengineering, defined it as "the fundamental rethinking and radical redesign of business *processes* to achieve dramatic improvements in critical measures of *performance* such as cost, quality, service and speed."[4] In other words, reengineering mainly focuses on corporate fitness—becoming lean and effective, a productive machine. The results to date have been poor.

In a survey of 99 completed reengineering initiatives undertaken in 1994, two-thirds were judged as producing mediocre, marginal, or failed results.[5] One of the principal reasons for this failure was the lack of attention given to the human dimension.[6] Half the companies that participated in the survey said the most difficult part of reengineering was dealing with the fear and anxiety in their organizations—not surprising when these companies were using reengineering to eliminate on average 21 percent of jobs. Thomas H. Davenport, one of the early proponents of reengineering, states that "Companies that embraced [reengineering] as the silver bullet are now looking for ways to rebuild the organization's torn social fabric."[7] The majority of organizations that undertook reengineering treated people as if they were redundant parts of the corporate machine. Less than half the companies that downsized have been rewarded with either short- or long-term increases in operating profits, and less than a third made rapid gains in productivity. Morale slumped in 72 percent of the companies that downsized.

Those who survive downsizing suffer as much as those who lose their jobs. They find themselves living in a climate of fear. There is no longer any trust in the organization. As fear increases, personal productivity and creativity decline. The stress becomes intolerable and the best people—those with strong employability—leave. Reengineering turned up the volume of fear in organizations and it was heard all over America.

When used appropriately, reengineering is a useful tool for building corporate fitness. It can enliven the corporate body by making it lean, supple, and fast. It keeps the systems and processes open, smooth, and efficient. However, instead of being used locally and sparingly as a tool for preventive maintenance, reengineering has become synonymous with radical surgery. The real issue is not with reengineering, but with the mind set that allows an organization's health to disintegrate to the point that reengineering in the form of radical surgery is seen as the only solution.

In The Living Company, Arie de Geus states that "Companies die because their managers focus on the economic activity of producing goods and services, and they forget that their organization's true nature is that of a community of humans."[8] To put the argument slightly differently, companies die because they concentrate on the physical aspects of their being (profit and growth) and ignore their emotional, mental, and spiritual needs. As Stephen Covey points out, highly effective people are highly effective because they keep all aspects of their lives in balance. This is also true of highly effective organizations.

Healthy organizations avoid early death or radical surgery by constantly monitoring their total well-being—not just their financial performance. They constantly review all aspects of corporate health and take corrective action before more serious interventions become necessary. They are like finely tuned athletes who take care of their bodies, their minds, and their spirits.

Reengineering in healthy companies addresses specific local issues. The numbers of people affected are small, and the reengineering is done in a caring way. Healthy companies are open and sensitive to their internal and external environments. They thrive and prosper because they grow and evolve, not just physically but emotionally, mentally, and spiritually too. As with humans, when insufficient attention is paid to the "softer" side of life, pain, suffering, and early death can easily result.

THE CORPORATE LIFE CYCLE

In Ichak Adizes' description of the 10 stages of a corporate life cycle[9] we see how the emotional aspects of company life affect the health of an organization.

Adizes suggests that the life cycle begins with *courtship*. Someone comes up with an exciting business idea, embraces the possibilities, views them from different angles, and then commits. The courtship ends when the entrepreneur assumes risk. The organization is born and *infancy* begins. The focus is no longer on ideas but on how to achieve results. The most urgent need is to create sales. There is a lot of rushing around looking for opportunities to build income. No one cares much about systems, paperwork, or procedures. Everyone is working long hours every day to make sales.

As the business takes off, the organization enters the all systems *Go-Go* stage. As the organization moves into a state of rapid growth, the founders believe that they can do no wrong. They want to be involved in all decisions. They spend their time running from one meeting to another. The *Go-Go* stage comes to an end when there is a realization that someone must bring order to the business. The organization enters the *adolescence* stage.

The founders hire a chief operation officer but have great difficulty handing over control. Divisions appear in the organization as the old-timers who lived through the chaos of infancy try to adjust to the new-timers who are attempting to bring systems and order to the business. Internal conflicts cause temporary distractions from the real work of the organization. Gradually, the organization takes on a more mature form and it enters into its *prime*. The "prime" stage is characterized by clarity of vision and purpose and a balance between flexibility and control. The organization continues to grow through satisfying customers' needs and creating innovative new products or services. New products are decentralized into new businesses. Eventually, the organization achieves *stability*. The stage of stability is characterized by steady growth and an increasing focus on short-term financial results. There is a subtle shift in emphasis from innovation to control. Marketing and development become targets for cost reduction. Gradually, the organization enters its *"aristocracy"* stage.

Status and self-esteem in the form of titles, office size, and a reserved parking space take on more and more importance. The focus is more on form and less on content. Getting on in the organization means pleasing the boss and not making waves. The organization begins to lose its entrepreneurial edge. It starts expanding through acquisitions rather than growing new businesses. When performance begins to decline, the organization enters the *recrimination* stage. The leaders may turn to reengineering to fix the organization. Scapegoats are identified and fired. Fear rules. Everyone is fighting for survival and trying to look good. Turf battles ensue. The death rattle of the organization shows up in falling share prices.

If organizations skip or survive the recrimination stage, then they enter the *bureaucracy* stage. The ratio of time and cost spent on support services compared with front-line services increases significantly. Procedure manuals become thicker and thicker. Everyone is swamped by paperwork. Control is everywhere. The chaos that nurtured creativity is eliminated. Leaders and managers forget about customers—they are too intent on empire building. Customers complain of the poor response times. Expenses grow faster than income. Eventually, the organization is so slow and ungainly that it is no longer able to feed itself. The share price drops and it dies.

THE ORGANIZATION AS A MACHINE

This description of the corporate life cycle shows that the physical survival of a company is intimately linked to the emotional issues of those who are leading and managing the company. The "personality" or "culture" of a company is one of the primary drivers of its success or failure. The reason why this fact gets little attention is that management theorists are still operating under the science-based metaphor of the organization as a machine. Margaret Wheatley describes the situation in the following terms:

> The engineering image we carry of ourselves has led to organizational lives in which we believe we can ignore the deep realities of human existence. We can ignore that people carry spiritual questions and quests into their work; we can ignore that people need love and acknowledgment; we can pretend that emotions are not part of our work lives; we can pretend that we don't have families, or health crises, or deep worries. In essence, we take the complexity of life and organize it away. . . . We trade uniqueness for control, and barter our humanness for petty performance measures.[10]

The metaphor of the organization as a machine could be termed the "physical" approach. It considers labor and materials as inputs and products and services as outputs. Management's job is to optimize the systems and processes so that they bring the largest financial reward. They do it by controlling productivity, efficiency, and quality. It is seen as an engineering problem to maximize output and minimize cost.

The Shifting Metaphor

In recent years, with the recognition of the importance of the knowledge worker, management theory has begun to stress the value of institutional learning. This has led to a shift in the predominant organizational metaphor from a "machine" to a "machine with a mind."

This shift to a machine with a mind makes a significant difference. If an organization has a mind, then it is a short step to recognizing that it has emotions too. This is what happens when an organization switches from learning about its external environment to also learning about its internal environment. When it starts to learn about itself, the pathway to the emotions opens up. This subtle shift—from intellectual learning to emotional learning—poses a strong challenge to the machine metaphor. Only people can think *and* feel. Organizations should no longer be regarded as machines but as living entities that display the full range of human emotions.

Increasingly, we will see learning organizations turn inward to discover themselves. This is inevitable, because external learning on its own will not give organizations the competitive advantage they seek. External learning about customer needs, markets, and competitors is important, but it does very little to address the internal cultural issues that prevent innovation, creativity, and productivity. People and organizations grow and develop only to the extent that they are willing to confront the emotional issues that separate them from their souls. Self-knowledge at a personal and organizational level is the only pathway to evolution and growth.

Daniel Goleman, in his best-seller *Emotional Intelligence,*[11] corroborates this position. He describes our two minds—one that thinks and one that feels; one that guides us in making rational choices and one that guides us in making intuitive decisions. Research shows that mental intelligence as measured by an intelligence quotient (IQ) has little relationship to how well we do at work. Of more importance is our emotional intelligence. This is the intelligence that helps us to discern and respond appropriately to the moods, temperaments, motivations, and desires of other people. When we turn our emotional intelligence inward, we are able to access our own feelings, discriminate among them, and draw upon them to guide our behavior. Emotional intelligence helps us to become self-motivated, to access our creativity, to be more productive, and to empathize with others. These are the abilities that build strong interpersonal relationships, promote a sense of community, and create productive partnerships. Successful companies of the future will be looking for managers and leaders who display strong emotional intelligence.

Emotional intelligence can be defined as the ability to sense, understand, and effectively apply the power and insight of emotions as a source of information, connection, and influence.[12] Emotional intelligence is feedback from the heart based on feelings and intuition. Intuition is the direct perception of truth independent of the reasoning process. Mental intelligence is feedback from the head based on reasoning and logic.

The feedback that our emotional intelligence gives us is values laden. It comes directly from the soul. It tells us about what we *feel* is right and what we *feel* is wrong. It is not based on the logic of the mind, but on the intuition of the heart. Decisions based on emotional intelligence make us feel good. They may also awaken the fears of the ego. When we have relied on our intellectual intelligence and then become aware of our emotional intelligence, we often find situations in which our mind tells us to do one thing and our heart tells us to do another. If we fail to listen to our emotional intelligence and take actions based purely on logic and reason, it is almost certain that we will regret our actions. The deeply held values that spring from the soul always lead to sound personal and business decisions. The reason is simple. The soul operates from the position of what is best for the good of the whole. The ego, on the other hand, operates from self-interest. The ego reasons from external data. The soul intuits from internal data.

THE ORGANIZATION AS A LIVING ENTITY

When an individual or an organization begins to care about the collective good, we enter the realm of spiritual values. Values such as trust, honesty, integrity, compassion, and sharing become very important. Organizations that operate with these values cannot be described as machines. They are living entities. They have physical, emotional, mental, and spiritual needs. Organizations that recognize themselves as living entities know that to achieve optimal health they must balance all of these needs.

Physical Well-Being

The physical well-being of an organization is determined by financial success. Profit, cash flow, return on assets, and shareholder value are the types of indicators that are used to measure physical well-being. Finance is to companies what water, food, and air are to human beings. It is the source of the energy that keeps companies alive. For the vast majority of companies, financial indicators are the only indicators they use to assess corporate health. The problem with financial indicators is that they focus on the past. They tell you nothing about the factors that govern future financial success—customer satisfaction, employee morale, internal cohesion, strategic alliances, innovation, and productivity. It is like driving a car with no gauges and only a rear-view mirror. You know about past performance but you don't know what speed you are currently going, or whether the engine is overheating, or how long your battery will last. An organization that sees itself as a living entity understands that long-term financial success is a function of the organization's physical, emotional, mental, and spiritual health. It constantly seeks to improve and monitor all these aspects.

Emotional Well-Being

The emotional well-being of an organization is determined by how good it feels about itself and the quality of its relationships. Corporate fitness—productivity, efficiency, and quality—and inter-personal relationships are the types of indicators that are used to measure emotional well-being. Employees at all levels need to feel they have a strong sense of friendship and connection to their co-workers and their supervisors. Without these relationships, they rarely contribute more than they are asked. Employees also need to feel a sense of fairness, equality, and recognition. They want responsible freedom and to take pride in their work. Bureaucracy, fear, exploitation, and poor working relationships between managers and staff are sure signs of poor emotional health. When companies are emotionally unhealthy, loyalty to co-workers is more important than loyalty to the company, and the quality of products and customer service deteriorates. An organization that sees itself as a living entity knows how important it is to feel good about itself. It strives to treat its employees as it would like to be treated itself. It understands that when you care for others, they care for you in return.

Mental Well-Being

The mental well-being of an organization is directly related to the openness of the company to both internal and external feedback. Learning is fundamental to survival in a competitive world. Without learning, employees are unable to progress and companies quickly become extinct. There are two aspects to mental well-being—learning that contributes to improvements in products and services and learning that contributes to internal growth. The first focuses on external market-based achievements, the second on internal culture-based improvements. Both internal growth and external achievement are important. External achievement fuels corporate self-esteem and morale, while internal growth fuels creativity. Participation and innovation are the types of indicators that measure mental well-being. Fostering creativity is far more important than fostering knowledge. Knowledge should be regarded as a springboard to creativity but not as a goal in itself. When knowledge is combined with rigid thinking, it blocks learning. Organizations that see themselves as living entities encourage employees to grow in both their personal and professional lives. Personal growth builds emotional intelligence and professional growth builds skills and intellect.

Spiritual Well-Being

The spiritual well-being of an organization is determined by its degree of internal and external connectedness. Cohesion, cooperation, partnering, strategic alliances, community involvement, and social responsibility are the types of indicators that are used to measure spiritual health. Internal connectedness occurs in organizations with strong values-driven cultures. When employees have a common identity, strive to achieve a common vision, and share the same values, they work together for the common good. They participate in collective learning and develop a strong sense of loyalty to company. External connectedness occurs when the organization forms strategic alliances with customers and suppliers and builds partnerships with the local community. The sense of internal and external connectedness is heightened when the company takes an ethical stance on issues that affect the well-being of society. Companies that see themselves as living beings focus on employee fulfillment. They know that when employees are encouraged by their supervisors to find meaning through their work, to make a difference in their local community, and to serve humanity or the planet, they bring forth the deepest levels of motivation, creativity, and loyalty. Spiritual well-being is the cultural glue that makes the difference between a good company and great company.

Emotional and spiritual motivation, not physical reengineering, provide the ultimate answers to increased productivity and creativity. What has been labeled the "soft stuff" by diehard scientific management theorists is about to become the next arena for corporate change. In the next century, the soft stuff will join ranks with the hard stuff in management theories. Managers and leaders will have to become comfortable discussing their values and behaviors and learn the differences between change, transformation, and evolution.

> **Change:** A different way of doing. Doing what we do now, but doing it in a more efficient, productive, or quality-enhancing way.

> **Transformation**: A different way of being. Involves changes at the deepest levels of beliefs, values, and assumptions. Results in fundamental shifts in personal and corporate behavior and organizational systems and structures. Transformation occurs in systems that are vulnerable, learn from mistakes, are open to the future, and can let go of the past and their rigid beliefs.

Evolution: A state of continual transformation and change. Involves constant adjustments in values, behaviors, and beliefs based on learning gained from internal and external feedback. Evolution most easily occurs in systems that are dedicated to learning, have internal cohesion based on multiple channels of open communication, and have a profound commitment to self-development.

The Dynamics of Transformation

There are five stages in the process of organizational and personal transformation (see Figure 1-1). The initial state can be described as *unawareness (A)*. In this state you are oblivious to the fact that you have a problem—you don't know what you don't know—you are unconsciously unskilled. You become aware of the problem through feedback from the internal or external environment. The feedback is usually uncomfortable and leads to a state of *awareness (B)*. Now you know you have a problem—you know what you don't know—you are consciously unskilled. When the feedback becomes very uncomfortable or threatening, you decide to take action. You examine the problem in detail and you see that it can be resolved only by *learning a new behavior (C)*. Shifting to this new way of being may involve facing and overcoming your fears. You gradually resolve the problem by *practicing the new behavior (D)*—you become consciously skilled in a new area. As the new behavior becomes part of your second nature, you develop a new way of being and your *values change (E)*—you become unconsciously skilled at dealing with this particular type of problem.[13] You are now ready for your next challenge (see Figure 1-1). Each time you successfully meet a challenge, you shift to a higher level of consciousness and the process repeats (A1 . . . E1, A2 . . . E2). This continual state of transformation is called evolution. As you learn to accept evolution as a new way of being, transformation occurs naturally. You find yourself open to feedback and can

**Five Stages of
Transformation**

**Evolution: A Continuous
State of Transformation**

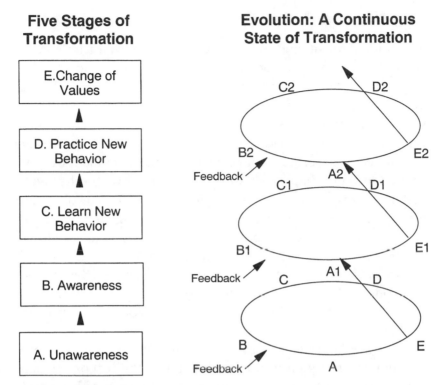

Figure 1-1
The Dynamics of the Transformation and Evolution of Consciousness

easily adapt your behaviors to achieve higher and higher states
of consciousness.

The Importance of Evolution

Organizational evolution is becoming increasingly important as
the pace of economic, technological, and social change accelerates.
In the twenty-first century, only companies that embrace evolution
will survive. Currently, the average life span of a multinational
corporation is about 40 to 50 years. We can expect this life span to
decrease as the pace of change accelerates. Evolution will be possible only for companies that are willing to engage in physical,
emotional, mental, and spiritual growth.

Long Life and Prosperity

Three independent studies have looked at the characteristics of successful companies, two of them from the perspective of longevity. In *Built to Last*,[14] James C. Collins and Jerry I. Porras present the results of a seven-year study of 18 long-lasting companies that have existed more than 45 years. These companies were widely admired, had a significant impact on the world, and maintained a superior level of financial performance. In their research, each of these companies is compared with other well-established organizations from similar sectors. The results were remarkable. Over a period of 64 years, the 18 long-lasting companies outperformed the comparison companies by a factor of 6 and outperformed the stock market by a factor of 15.

In *The Living Company*,[15] Arie de Geus examines the key factors contributing to corporate longevity by referring to a Royal/Dutch Shell study of 27 international companies incorporated before 1913.

In *The 8 Practices of Exceptional Companies*,[16] Jac Fitz-Enz presents the results of four years of research into the best practices of human asset management in companies that displayed high profitability and employee retention.

The results of these three studies are extremely similar. The key characteristics of long-lasting companies that have superior financial performance are summarized as follows.

- A strong, positive, values-driven culture
- A lasting commitment to learning and self-renewal
- Continual adaptation based on feedback from internal and external environments
- Strategic alliances with internal and external partners, customers, and suppliers
- A willingness to take risks and experiment
- A balanced, values-based approach to measuring performance that includes such factors as:
  —Corporate survival (financial results)
  —Corporate fitness (efficiency, productivity, and quality)

— Collaboration with suppliers and customers
— Continuous learning and self-development (evolution)
— Organizational cohesion and employee fulfillment
— Corporate contribution to the local community and society

The six characteristics of long-lasting successful companies are similar to those of a living entity that is evolving and growing. The basic reason why companies find it difficult to develop these characteristics is that they operate from the mental model of the organization as a *machine*. More and more organizations are making the transition to the mental model of a *machine with a mind*, but very few have made it to the model of the organization as a living entity. Consequently, most companies seek only to satisfy their physical and emotional needs. Some companies are attempting to satisfy their mental needs by becoming learning organizations, but they are mostly focusing on learning for achievement. They have not recognized the importance of learning for internal growth. To evolve and grow, organizations need to focus on self-knowledge and self-renewal, recognize the long-term futility of corporate self-interest, and embrace the common good.

In the following chapter, we will examine where the philosophy self-interest is leading corporations; why this direction is unsustainable; why there is hope for the future; and how the values shift that is beginning to take root in business is good for the organizations, good for employees, good for society, and good for the environment.

Notes

1. James C. Collins and Jerry I. Porras, *Built to Last: Successful Habits of Visionary Companies* (New York: HarperBusiness, 1994).

2. John P. Kotter and James L. Heskett, *Corporate Culture and Performance* (New York: The Free Press, 1992), p. 89.

3. James C. Collins and Jerry I. Porras, *Built to Last: Successful Habits of Visionary Companies* (New York: HarperBusiness, 1994), p. 28.

4. Michael Hammer and J. Champy, *Reengineering the Corporation: A Manifesto for Business Revolution* (New York: HarperCollins, 1994).

5. *Fast Company Magazine*, Premiere Issue, *Why Re-engineering Failed*, Thomas H. Davenport, 1995, pp. 69–74.

6. *Wall Street Journal*, November 26, 1996.

7. Ibid.

8. Arie de Geus, *The Living Company: Habits for Survival in a Turbulent Business Environment* (Boston: Harvard Business School Press, 1997).

9. *Inc.* Magazine, Adapted from *The Pursuit of Prime*, by Ichak Adizes, October 1996.

10. Margaret Wheatley, *The New Story Is Ours to Tell*, Perspectives on Business and Global Change, Vol. II, No. 2 (World Business Academy, June 1997).

11. Daniel Goleman, *Emotional Intelligence* (New York: Bantam Books, 1995), p. 9.

12. Robert K. Cooper and Ayman Sawaf, *Executive EQ: Emotional Intelligence in Leadership & Organizations* (New York: Grosset/Putnam), p. xiii.

13. I am grateful to Gita Bellin from Australia in bringing to my awareness the concept of being consciously and unconsciously skilled, and unskilled.

14. James C. Collins and Jerry I. Porras, *Built to Last: Successful Habits of Visionary Companies* (New York: HarperBusiness, 1994).

15. Arie de Geus, *The Living Company: Habits for Survival in a Turbulent Business Environment* (Boston: Harvard Business School Press, 1997).

16. Jac Fitz-Enz, *The 8 Exceptional Practices of Exceptional Companies: How Great Organizations Make the Most of Their Human Assets* (New York: AMACOM, 1997).

2

The Common Good

Many companies around the world believe that they have a moral duty to respond to global problems such as Third World poverty, the deterioration of the natural environment, and endless trade battles. But few have actually realized that their survival actually depends on their response. To put it simply global companies have no future if the earth has no future.
—RYUZABURO KAKU, HONORARY CHAIRMAN OF THE BOARD, CANON

Laissez-faire capitalism holds that the common good is best served by the uninhibited pursuit of self-interest. Unless it is tempered by the recognition of a common interest that ought to take precedence over particular interests, our present system is liable to break down.
—GEORGE SOROS, FINANCIER

Throughout history, survival and growth have been at the center of the preoccupations of groups of people united around a common identity and purpose—first in tribes; then in clans, kingdoms, and nations; and more recently in corporations. Organizations are becoming the new communities of the world—bringing together people around a common purpose with shared values that transcends cultural, racial, and national boundaries. For the sake of survival and growth, corporations are giving up their national identities to achieve a global presence. Transnational organizations are uniting people under a single corporate culture. Companies such as Nestlé of Switzerland, Thomson of Canada, Solvay of Belgium, Cable and Wireless of

Britain, Philips of The Netherlands, and Volvo of Sweden have more than 70 percent of their assets in foreign countries.[1]

Whereas societal cultures are based on value systems that draw from tradition, religion, and racial heritage, corporate cultures are almost exclusively based on value systems that are economically focused. Because of the singular focus on money, "business" has become the most powerful institution on the planet. The annual spending of companies such as General Motors, Exxon, Ford, IBM, General Electric, and Mobil is similar to or exceeds government spending in Canada and the majority of the governments of Europe.[2] Of the world's 100 largest economies, 51 are global corporations. Only 49 are nations. The economy of Mitsubishi is larger than that of Indonesia, the world's fourth most populous country and a land of enormous wealth.[3] The combined sales of the world's top 200 corporations are equal to 28 percent of the world gross domestic product.[4] The same 200 corporations employ only 18.8 million people, less than one-third of 1 percent of the world's population.[5]

CORPORATE AUTOCRACY

Unlike most governments, whose leaders are democratically elected and accountable to the people they serve, corporations and their leaders are accountable only to themselves and a relatively small group of wealthy shareholders. In the United States, 77 percent of shareholder wealth is owned by only 5 percent of the population. Included in this 5 percent are the top echelons of management who are partly compensated through company shares. The principal preoccupation of this population of shareholders is return on their capital. In 1993, 96 percent of so-called investment was parasitic[6]—investors betting on stocks as if they were horses. Only 4 percent of the sale of stock was in new equity—productive investment.[7] Rarely are the gamblers in stocks committed to the long-term future of the companies. They buy and sell whenever they can make a profit. They tend not to care about the well-being of employees or the communities in which the companies are located.[8] The overwhelming majority of productive investment, 82 percent, is made by companies themselves plowing back their earnings. The remaining 14 percent of productive investment comes from borrowing.[9]

In an article in *Business Week*, Bruce Nussbaum and Judith H. Dobrzynski state that "The corporation, perhaps more than most institutions, is based on a series of myths. Managers serve owners. . . . Shareholders elect representatives to the board of directors and the free market disciplines winners and losers. All the myths have a purpose: to make us believe the corporation is accountable. The truth of the matter is that corporations have generally been benevolent autocracies for decades." The CEO or a few top executives exercise control in the great majority of enterprises. Consequently, the philosophy of most corporations is not distinguishable from the personal ambitions of the CEO. For many, these ambitions primarily focus on increasing their own personal net worth.

Most of the increased profit margins in America over the past 50 years have been skewed toward senior executives. In 1953, executive compensation was the equivalent of 22 percent of corporate profit. By 1987 it was 61 percent. Between 1979 and 1988 the salaries of chief executive officers increased from 29 to 93 times the income of the average manufacturing worker.[10] U.S. corporate executives receive salaries up to 225 times those of the lowest paid employees. According to the Institute for International Economics, during the past two decades the ratio of wages of the top 10 percent of workers to those of the bottom 10 percent rose from 360 percent to 525 percent for men and 380 percent to 430 percent for women. The income gap between the best paid and worst paid of American workers is now the most extreme among the world's 25 advanced industrial nations.

History shows that this is a potentially dangerous situation. Cultures that concentrate economic power in a rich elite who are not accountable to the people generally do not survive. The lack of accountability in the world of business has reached pandemic proportions. The physical environment has deteriorated to such an extent that life on the planet is threatened. Mass poverty is undermining the social stability of many countries, and millions of young adults are giving up hope of having a meaningful future. The following quotation from a "Generation Xer" (one born between 1965 and 1975) is typical of the deeply felt malaise. "I see the reality of deforestation, ozone depletion, and watershed contamination of our planet amid the interminable political turmoil in the world at large. These are vital issues, and they will affect me before they affect my children. How are we to live our lives in the knowledge that if we do not derail our current actions the world will not be habitable in our lifetimes?"

Environmental Degradation

Since the origin of complex life forms on Earth, there have been five mass extinctions. The last occurred 65 million years ago. During some of these periods as much as 96 percent of all species were wiped out. The pattern of extinctions and renewals is similar. After each collapse, the survivors thoroughly exploit the new ecological opportunities. Life forms thrive and diversity increases. Then comes the next extinction. A sawtooth pattern comprising a sharp downward slope (extinction) followed by a slow upward slope (recovery) is repeated time and again.[11]

According to paleoanthropologist Richard Leakey, the pressures of modern society are leading us into the sixth extinction.[12] A new downward slope began at the start of the industrial revolution. It has been estimated that as much as 50 percent of the world's species will be extinct within three decades. Unlike previous extinctions, which were caused by global disasters of natural origin such as the impact of asteroids or massive volcanic eruptions, the present extinction is happening because of the unrelenting growth of human populations and the way humanity is exploiting the planet. For the first time in history we are experiencing the environmental impact of economic activity and human population at a global level. The possible extent of this impact is revealed in The World Conservation Union (IUCN) 1996 Red List of Threatened Animals. The list reveals that 25 percent of mammal species and 11 percent of bird species are classified as being threatened with extinction. It is also estimated that 20 percent of reptiles, 25 percent of amphibians, and 34 percent of fish-es (mostly freshwater) are also threatened.[13]

Some environmentalists believe that the burden of pollution is rapidly reaching a point where it will destabilize the world's food chains and ecosystems.[14] The loss of so many species in recent decades lends much credibility to this assertion. Few would argue that current industrial practices and consumption patterns are sustainable. Although there may be broad agreement on the environmental problems facing humanity, there is less agreement on the solutions. The industrial nations are unwilling to give up their consumptive lifestyle and the developing nations are unwilling to stop capitalizing on their natural resources.

At a World Bank conference on Ethics and Spiritual Values in Development, Timothy Worth, the United States Under-Secretary of State for Global Affairs, linked environmental destruction with economic survival. He put it this way: "The economy is a wholly owned subsidiary of the environment. When the environment is finally forced to file for bankruptcy because its resource base has been polluted, degraded, and irretrievably compromised, then the economy will go bankrupt with it."[15]

At the same World Bank conference, Willis Harman, cofounder of the World Business Academy, asked the question, "What is it that has to change in order for sustainable develop-ment to be really possible?" He replied: "It is not so much indi-vidual values we are talking about. Individually, both rich and poor express wholesome values. It is, rather, the values embedded in the institutions of business and finance that are the problem. People feel a discrepancy between what they know in their hearts is right and what they feel forced to do to support their organiza-tion's values and goals."[16] We are all accountable for what is hap-pening to our planet. It is time we became responsible too.

Social Inequality

Across the world, growing economic inequalities and increasing unemployment are causing social unrest. Survival has become a daily concern for hundreds of millions of people all over the world. It is clear that the rules that govern our global economic system are creating disparities that favor the rich and injure the poor.

The extent of the global polarization of wealth was starkly illustrated in 1997 by an article in *Forbes* magazine.[17] It listed 447 billionaires whose combined net worth was roughly equivalent to the annual income of the poorest half of the world's population (2.7 billion people). The United Nations Development Programme estimates that approximately three-quarters of the world's population are economically insecure. Economic disparities are also increasing in the rich countries. In the United States, for example, during the past few decades the richest 1 percent of the population has doubled its proportion of the national wealth from 20 to 40 percent.

One of the results of these inequalities is an increase in global unemployment. According to the International Labor Office, global unemployment and underemployment are higher today than they were at the height of the great depression of the 1930s.[18] In *The End of Work*, Jeremy Rifkin shows the important role technology has had in shifting work from agriculture to manufacturing and from manufacturing to the service sector. He shows that, in every sector, human labor is being replaced by machines.

The downward trend in the demand for unskilled labor suggests that global unemployment figures will continue to rise. The situation in Europe is particularly disturbing. Double-digit unemployment rates have become increasingly common. Even with the low assumption of a 3 percent growth in the labor force of the industrialized world over the next 30 years, the World Bank says that deep questions remain about what can be done to reduce unemployment.[19] In most of the developing world, where the labor force is expected to grow by 56 percent from 2.1 billion to 3.2 billion over the next 30 years, the prospects for a commensurate growth in employment are bleak.

Author Paul Hawken points to a significant link between the issue of unemployment and the consumption of the world's natural resources. He states: "We have spent the last century, and most of us the last decades, working our tails off in order to make fewer and fewer people more and more productive using systems of manufacturing, distribution, and communication that use more and more resources. We are doing all this precisely at a time when we have less and less resources and more and more people."[20]

GLOBAL SURVIVAL

We are facing a situation in which increasing inequities and rising unemployment are creating worldwide social disintegration and increasing consumption of the Earth's natural resources and growing pollution are destroying our global environment. As the twenty-first century approaches, the issue of survival is becoming pervasive. Corporate autocracy and the current value system of the free market are destroying the life support systems of the planet and condemning hundreds of millions of people to poverty. We are living in a world where the natural resources of the Earth are being plundered for corporate profits and where the toxic waste from our factories is causing species to become extinct at a faster rate than ever before. Environmental destruction and social disintegration are capturing the headlines around the world.

George Soros, who has made millions of dollars speculating on the financial markets, echoes these thoughts. He states,

> I fear that untrammeled intensification of laissez-faire capitalism and the spread of market values into all areas of life is endangering our open and democratic society. The main enemy of the open society, I believe, is no longer the communist threat but the capitalist threat. Too much competition and too little cooperation can cause intolerable inequities and instability. The doctrine of laissez-faire capitalism holds that the common good is best served by the uninhibited pursuit of self-interest. Unless it is tempered by the recognition of a common interest that ought to take precedence over particular interests, our present system . . . is liable to break down.[21]

Self-interest and the single-minded pursuit of accumulation of wealth lie at the heart of our current crisis. Fueled by greed, businesses all over the world are engaged in the wholesale exploitation of the Earth and its people. What is extraordinary is that they are doing it in collusion with society. Tens of millions of fair-minded citizens, concerned over the future of their families, support this situation because they believe their economic survival depends on it. Many people have allowed their deeper values to become so blinkered by dollars that they are unable to see that they are participating in collective suicide. Many fail individually, and as organizations and nations, to acknowledge the economic and environmental interconnectedness of humanity and our planet's natural support systems. So many of us are focused on creating personal wealth that we are unwilling to admit that our personal ambitions are contributing to the pollution of the Earth, the exploitation of its peoples, and the disintegration of our communities.

We are living in an untenable situation. But all is not lost. From within the depths of crises spring the seeds of transformation. A global shift in consciousness is taking place that will forever change the operating rules of society and the role of corporations.

A HISTORICAL PERSPECTIVE

My optimism is based on the history of the evolution of consciousness. The true value of the study of history is to be found in the values that precipitated changes and transformations. Historic events are the footprints of evolution of human consciousness. Behind every historical event lies a statement of values. Throughout history, the common good has always emerged as the primary motivating force whenever the survival, prosperity, or happiness of the masses was threatened.

When human beings appeared on Earth, they quickly learned that their chances of survival increased significantly if they lived in extended family groups. Men hunted while the women gathered fruits and brought up their young. The clan survived by working together for the common good. They had shared beliefs and common values. As populations increased, clan survival was threatened as competition for territory grew. To protect their lands, clans with similar cultures joined together to form tribes. Tribalism became the dominant form of cultural identity. For the sake of survival, the belief systems and values of clans coalesced into a shared tribal culture. A close dependence developed between the security and prosperity of the clan and the security and prosperity of the tribe. As tribes thrived and grew, competition for land and resources increased. Wars broke out over "ownership" of territory. Survival was intimately linked to the accumulation of land. Those with the most fertile and largest tracts of land had the best chance of survival. Armies were formed to protect tribal lands and expand into new territories. The strongest tribes subjugated the weaker tribes, and they began to live together under the authority of a monarch. Nations began to form. Tribal boundaries were replaced by constitutional boundaries. The era of monarchies began.

Compared with the era of tribalism, the era of monarchies was short-lived. The reason for the downfall of monarchies was that too much power was vested in too few. While the masses suffered in deprivation and poverty, kings and queens, protected by their armies, felt safe to exploit their subjects and indulge their self-interest. They had little concern for the common good. Gradually, in one country after another, the people came together to limit the powers of their monarchs or throw them out altogether. They replaced them with governance structures that attempted to bring equality and freedom to the masses. There was a new melding of beliefs around shared values that became codified in national laws. These new modes of governance embraced openness and transparency and delegated decision-making authority to groups of individuals chosen by the people. They protected citizens from internal tyrants and outside threats and set up systems to care for the old, the frail, and the sick. The principle of the common good became established as the essential characteristic of a democratic nation-state.

The democratic nation-state is a relatively new concept in modern history. It began to take form in the seventeenth century with the English Civil War and later in the eighteenth, nineteenth, and twentieth centuries when populations came together to overthrow exigent and self-serving kings, queens, dictators, and colonial powers. Democracy gained even more momentum in the last 50 years. Almost all the world's former colonies have moved to self-rule. More recently, in the last 25 years, dictatorships collapsed in Greece, Spain, Portugal, and in most Latin American countries. Taiwan and South Korea have also become more democratic.

The reason democracy is increasing so quickly is that the people of the world are taking back their power. Wherever there is oppression, wherever the masses are exploited, and wherever greed is rampant, people are coming together to oust their leaders. The Russians first rejected their monarchy and then communism because neither structure served the common good. White South Africans rejected apartheid for the same reason. They voluntarily agreed to give up self-interest to support the collective good. When one views history from this perspective, one can clearly trace the shift in values that represents the evolution of human consciousness—a shift from self-interest to the common good.

Lessons from History

This brief review of values in history has some sobering lessons for corporations. First, the most successful groups of people have always been those who developed value systems that created security, stability, and prosperity for all. The subjugation of self-interest to the common good is the hallmark of a successful long-term culture. Second, history shows that when large groups are continually exploited by a rich elite, the people will inevitably find ways to undermine those in power to create a democratic culture in which benefits are more equally shared. Third, when faced with threats of survival, people join together in strategic alliances to overcome the external threat for the sake of the common good. At this point in history, the fundamental problem is not the breakdown of society or the destruction of life support systems—it is the inability of institutions and corporations to embrace values that support the common good.

VALUES SHIFT

When the economist E. F. Schumaker was asked "What can we do?" he said, "The answer is as simple as it is disconcerting: we can, each of us, work to put our own house in order." It is time for each of us to recognize that our own survival and the survival of our children depend on our accepting personal responsibility for the future. We must see humanity and the environment as they really are—totally interdependent and wholly interconnected. We must recognize that the decisions we make individually, and in our organizations and governments, have repercussions around the globe. We must not be afraid to take our highest values to work. It is time for each of us to engage fully in transforming the values of business.

There are millions of people around the world embracing this new responsibility. They are turning from *"What's in it for me?"* as their unconscious world view, to consciously embracing *"What's best for the common good?"* Many of these people are business leaders. Companies around the world are beginning to recognize that their future is intimately linked to peace, prosperity for all, and environmental stewardship.

The Caux Round Table of business leaders from Europe, Japan, and the U. S. developed a set of business principles known as the Caux Principles. These Principles focus on the importance of global corporate responsibility in reducing social and economic threats to world peace and stability. The corporate leaders believe moral values are a necessity in business decision-making and that businesses have a role to play in improving the lives of all their customers, employees, and shareholders by sharing with them the wealth they have created. The Caux Principles were founded on the ethical ideals of *kyosei* and human dignity. *Kyosei* is a Japanese word meaning "spirit of cooperation." It encourages individuals and organizations to live and work together for the common good. It was first introduced in Japan in 1987 by Ryuzaburo Kaku, President of Canon from 1977 to 1989, and is now honorary chairman and a member of the Caux Round Table.[22] A company that is practicing kyosei establishes harmonious relations with its customers, its suppliers, its competitors, the governments with which it interacts, and the natural environment. For the past 10 years, it has become Canon's most cherished principle. Ryuzaburo Kaku believes that, "If corporations run their businesses with the sole aim of gaining more market share or earning more profits, they may well lead the world into economic, environmental, and social ruin. But if they work together for the common good they can bring food to the poor, peace to war-torn areas and renewal to the natural world. It is our obligation as business leaders to join together to build a foundation for world peace and prosperity."

Another business leader who takes personal responsibility for his work force to heart is Aaron Feuerstein. When a fire destroyed his Malden Mills textile manufacturing plant, he continued paying his 3,000 workers even though they were unable to return to work for several months. Feuerstein believes he has a responsibility to his employees and to the community. Feuerstein's reward was a loyal and motivated work force that increased its output by 75 percent a few months after they returned to work.

A study by James E. Austin, professor of business administration at the Harvard Business School, shows that 82 percent of 316 CEOs of Fortune 500 companies served on nonprofit boards, the vast majority on more than one.[23] When asked why they undertook this work, the majority replied that they volunteered primarily because of their belief in the mission of the nonprofit and their sense of responsibility to the community. Austin reports that, "They found that their participation exposed them to new contacts and ideas, and allowed them to develop managerial and leadership skills in ways that were not available in their job settings." A growing number of companies are encouraging their junior and senior managers to volunteer. They find it is an innovative way to develop skills in leadership, mission and policy formulation, and interpersonal management skills.[24]

Austin's study also surveyed 9,835 Harvard Business School graduates to gauge their involvement in nonprofit organizations. Sixty-five percent of respondents between the ages of

25 and 29 reported that they were significantly engaged in the social sector.[25]

Companies are also getting involved in volunteerism. A mentoring program for children at risk in city areas has attracted the attention of several large corporations. Disney has promised a million hours of voluntary service from its employees. Kmart will allow its 2,150 stores to be used as safe havens for children at risk. Timberland will allow its employees to do 40 hours of service a year on company pay and company time. Coca-Cola has pledged money to train volunteers to act as mentors to disadvantaged children.[26]

Some companies are now offering volunteer work as an employee perk. At Wild Oats Markets Inc., it is included in the employee handbook. Wild Oats pays employees 1 hour of charity time for every 40 hours of work. At beverage maker Nantucket Nectars, part of their credo includes "promoting community participation." The program is so popular that the company is having a difficult time keeping up with its employees' varied interests.[27] In September 1995, a consortium of 21 major corporations pledged $100 million for a family care aid program in 56 cities. The money is being used to fund day care centers for children and elderly people and improve the skills of the care providers.

Paul Ray estimates that 44 million people in America have embraced this new consciousness and that this number is increasing.[28] His "American Lives" survey revealed that there are now three predominant world views. Just one generation ago, social researchers could find only two. The new culture, which he describes as the Integral Culture, is rapidly gaining on the traditionalist and the modernist world views. The Integral Culture is characterized by values such as ecological sustainability, global awareness, equality, altruism, and a well-developed social conscience. Those belonging to this group firmly reject materialism, consumerism, and the modern business culture.

This is not the only group that is rejecting the current philosophy of business. A 1996 *Business Week* poll found that 95 percent of 1,000 adult Americans reject the idea that a corporation's only role is to make money. Seventy-one percent said that business had too much power and is morally responsible for the country's woes. Fifty-eight percent of executives strongly agreed that corporations have a responsibility to address work-family issues, diversity, equal rights, and the environment, but only 14 percent agreed that the corporate leaders are doing a good job at this. The Cone/Roper Cause-Related Marketing Trends Report of 1997 found that 76 percent of consumers would be likely to switch brands associated with a good cause if price and quality were equal. This figure is up from 66 percent in 1993. The report also found that 76 percent of consumers said they would not only switch brands but also switch retailers to support a good cause. This figure is up from 62 percent in 1993.

Corporate Social Responsibility

Corporate social responsibility is becoming increasingly important for workers. A survey at Polaroid and Gillette in August 1996 by the Center for Corporate Community Relations found that 84 percent of their employees believe a company's image in the community is important. Fifty-four percent said it was *very* important. Those who feel the company has a strong community presence feel loyal to the company and positive about themselves. Maceo Sloan, CEO of Sloan Financing Group, says that his company's bottom line is that "companies that are indifferent or callous to their social responsibilities are, by definition, poor business people who will not maximize the creation of shareholder wealth."

Tomorrow's managers also regard social responsibility as a high priority. According to a study of 2,100 students at 50 graduate business programs conducted by Students for Responsible Business, 79 percent of MBAs think a company has to take into consideration the impact it has on society in terms of the environment, equal opportunities, work and family relationships, and community involvement. Fifty percent said they would accept a lower salary to work for a "very socially responsible" company. Forty-three percent claimed that they would not work for a company that wasn't socially responsible.[29]

Increasingly, the parameters by which we define success will become the same parameters by which we define evolution. They will become spiritual and collective rather than material and individual. For example, can we really say that we are successful if we are living in a large house in a fine neighborhood that has to be guarded and secured by gates and high walls? Can we really say we are successful if nine out of ten people will never be able to enjoy the security, comfort, and well-being that we enjoy? Can we really say we are successful if we contaminate the air we breathe and pollute the water we drink? Clearly, none of these situations will give us the security, prosperity, and happiness we are looking for. And yet, we continue to focus narrowly on the material dimensions of success, while all around us the signs of failure grow like shadows as the sun moves past high noon and descends into night.

All of these issues go beyond the type of pain that individuals normally experience. They represent the collective pain of society and humanity. It is clear that the societal assumptions about what creates security, prosperity, and happiness are severely flawed. While they give the appearance of working for the small numbers of rich, they fail to work for vast numbers of others. The flaw in our assumptions is that individual security, prosperity, and happiness can be achieved through paradigms that focus on pure self-interest. Our modern world experience shows this is no longer true. All humanity and the planet's life support systems are so intricately linked that long-lasting security, prosperity, and happiness will be achievable only if we focus on the common good. The fundamental issue for the next century will become not the creation of wealth but the sharing of wealth. The only way corporations will survive the twenty-first century is by fully embracing what is economically, socially, and environmentally best for the common good.

In *The 100 Best Companies to Work for in America*,[30] Robert Levering and Milton Moskowitz provide details of how companies are recognizing that it is good business to share ownership and profits, to care for the physical and emotional needs of employees and their families, to provide opportunities for personal growth and advancement, and to support the local community and serve humanity.

What the staff of the "100 Best Companies" appreciated most was the feeling of community. People want to experience a sense of belonging built on trust, and they want to bring their highest values to work. Author Scott Peck says: "Introduce genuine community into your business, and you will guarantee its ethical integrity." [31]

Not only does *The 100 Best Companies to Work for in America* show that companies are living by higher values, it also shows that the number of such companies is increasing. Of the 100 companies that were chosen for the first edition in 1984, only 55 made it through to the second edition in 1993. The authors point out that the 45 companies that didn't make it are still good places to work. They have simply been replaced by better companies. Competition to be one of the best companies to work for in America is increasing!

William M. Mercer's Work/Life and Diversity Initiatives Benchmarking survey shows that a growing number of corporations are focusing on the common good. The survey conducted in 1996 found that 86 percent of the 800 companies said they could not compete in the 90s work arena without addressing work/life and diversity issues. More than half of the survey respondents believe work/life programs positively affect employee morale, attendance, productivity, and recruitment.[32] They also have a positive impact on the bottom line. In *Creating High Performance Organizations*[33] The Minnesota Center for Corporate Responsibility details the advantages to employers of work/life strategies. They:

- Reduce the cost of hiring, training, and development
- Help retain talented workers
- Increase productivity by reducing absenteeism, stress, and distractions
- Increase employee loyalty to the organization
- Build a positive image in the marketplace
- Strengthen family ties and build a healthier society

The U.S. government is getting into the act. The Malcolm Baldrige National Quality Award, established by Congress in 1987, is the highest level of recognition for performance excellence that a U.S. company can receive. The main focus of the reward is competitiveness through quality. The award is based on a number of factors that focus on values-based management. These factors include:

- How clearly an organization's leadership defines its company's values
- How senior management addresses social responsibilities and community involvement
- How the organization manages and develops its relationship with customers
- How the work force is empowered to its fullest potential and aligned with company objectives
- How the organization builds and maintains an environment supporting performance excellence, full participation, personal and organizational growth
- How the organization manages and develops its supplier partnering processes

Competition for the award is extremely keen. Past winners of the award include companies such as AT&T, Corning, Federal Express, IBM, Texas Instruments, and Xerox.

It is clear that in the coming years organizations will need to shift their attention to satisfying not only their physical needs but also their emotional, mental, and spiritual needs. During the past few decades the emphasis has been on providing increased material welfare for employees. In the next century, the emphasis will be on providing emotional, mental, and spiritual support. People will want to work in organizations that allow them to bring their highest values to work, give them an opportunity to make a positive difference in the world, and encourage them to become all they can become. Surveys show that as workers feel a sense of satisfaction and a belief that their work is meaningful, the motivational influence of salary and benefits becomes less important.[34]

When people find meaningful work, they tap into their deepest levels of intuition and creativity. This is good for them and good for the organization too.

A recent Gallup Poll of 55,000 workers supports this conclusion.[35] The survey found that four attitudes, taken together, correlate strongly with higher profits. The four attitudes are: Workers feel they are given the opportunity to do what they do best every day; they believe their opinions count; they believe their fellow workers are committed to quality; and they've made a direct connection between their work and the company's mission.

The next chapter delves more deeply into how an organization can unleash the highest levels of creativity and productivity of its employees and what visionary organizations can do to encourage employee fulfillment.

Notes

1. Based on 1995 index of transnationality published by United Nations Conference on Trade and Development. The ratio is based on the average of a companies' foreign assets to total assets, foreign sales to total sales, and foreign employment to total employment.

2. Ralph Estes, *Tyranny of the Bottom Line* (San Francisco: Berrett-Koehler, 1996), p. 89.

3. Sarah Anderson and John Cavanagh, *The Top 200: The Rise of the Global Corporate Power* (Washington, D.C.: Institute for Policy Studies, 1996). Referenced in David Korten's article "A Market-Based Approach to Corporate Responsibility," *Perspectives on Business and Global Change*, Vol. 11, No. 2 (World Business Academy, June 1997).

4. Ibid.

5. Ibid.

6. Thornton Parker, "Today's Stock Investment Dilemma," *Perspectives on Business and Global Change*, Vol. 11, No. 2 (World Business Academy, June 1997).

7. Ralph Estes, *Tyranny of the Bottom Line* (San Francisco: Berrett-Koehler, 1996), p. 50.

8. Ibid.

9. Ibid.

10. Jeremy Rifkin, *The End of Work* (New York: G. P. Putnam's Sons, 1995), p.173.

11. Richard Leakey and Roger Lewin, *Origins Reconsidered* (New York: Doubleday, 1992), p. 354.

12. Ibid., p. 353.

13. The full text of the Red List can be acquired via The World Conservation Union's Web site: http://www.iucn.org/themes/ssc/index.html

14. *World Resources: A Guide to the Global Environment 1994–95*, World Resources Institute in collaboration with the United Nations Environment Programme and The United Nations Development Programme (New York: Oxford University Press, 1994), pp. 213–214.

15. *Ethical and Spiritual Values: Promoting Environmentally Sustainable Development*, Editors, Richard Barrett and Ismail Serageldin, Environmentally Sustainable Development Proceedings Series No. 12, 1996, p. 30.

16. Ibid., p. 6.

17. Johnathan T. Davis, *Forbes Richest People: The Forbes Annual Profile of the World's Wealthiest Men and Women* (New York: John Wiley & Sons, 1997).

18. International Labor Organization, *The World Employment Situation, Trends and Prospects* (Geneva: International Labour Office, 1994).

19. *World Development Report 1995: Workers in an Integrating World* (Washington, D.C.: World Bank, 1995), p. 120.

20. In Context: A Journal of Hope, Sustainability, and Change, No. 41. Interview with Paul Hawken. Bainbridge Island, WA.

21. G. Soros, "The Capitalist Threat," *Perspectives*, Vol. 11, No. 3 (World Business Academy, 1997).

22. Ryuzaburo Kaku, "The path of Kyosei," *Harvard Business Review*, July–August 1997, pp. 55–63.

23. Judith A. Ross, "Community service: More rewarding than you think," *Harvard Business Review*, July–August 1997, p. 14.

24. Ibid.

25. Ibid.

26. "The Worker and the Volunteer," Lexington Column, *The Economist*, April 26, 1997.

27. Susan Greco, "Volunteering: The new employee perk," *Inc.* Magazine, September 1997, p. 116.

28. Paul H. Ray, *The Rise of Integral Culture*, Monograph published by the Institute of Noetic Sciences Review.

29. *Positive Leadership*, Vol. 1, No.1.

30. Robert Levering and Milton Moskowitz, *The 100 Best Companies to Work for in America* (New York: Doubleday, 1993).

31. Business Ethics, interview with M. Scott Peck, March/April, 1994.

32. For a free copy of the survey, call William M. Mercer (502) 561–4759.

33. For a free copy call (612) 962–4120.

34. David C. Trott, *Fluor Daniel: Results of spiritual well-being study*, Department of Educational Administration, The University of Austin, Texas, 1995.

35. Linda Grant, "Happy workers, high returns," *Fortune* Magazine, January, 1998, p. 81.

3

Motivation, Creativity, and Innovation

There has never been a better time for a business revolution and quest for new heights than today. This is not a revolution of anarchists, however, but of activists and innovators: it's about daring to open the flow of ideas and propose that which has never been considered before; about tearing down walls between what was previously an independent unit; about fostering a climate of knowledge sharing within the group that is conducive to creativity and value creation.

—BJÖRN WOLRATH, FORMER PRESIDENT AND CEO, SKANDIA

The key to success is to get out into the store and listen what the associates have to say. It's terribly important for everyone to get involved. Our best ideas come from clerks and stockboys.

—SAM WALTON, FOUNDER, WAL-MART

There are many things we cannot predict about where the current wave of change will take us. We can, however, be sure that innovative companies and societies will be the ones that thrive.

—PAUL ROMER, PROFESSOR OF ECONOMICS, GRADUATE SCHOOL OF BUSINESS, STANFORD UNIVERSITY

The most successful species on the planet are those that continuously adapt to their changing environment. Evolution has never been an exercise in strategic planning but a series of continual adjustments based on a sensitivity to the internal and external factors that affect an organism's chances of survival. For the human species the most significant threat to survival has been competition. For thousands of years, humanity's primary response to the threat of competition has been to wipe out or assimilate the "enemy." Its secondary response has been to gain advantage by being more innovative and creative. We are now living in a time when competition for survival, in an economic sense, has reached global proportions. It has become impossible to wipe out or assimilate all the "enemies." Survival is no longer an issue of superior power or force, but an issue of superior creativity. The biggest challenge facing organizations is how to build a culture that encourages the highest levels of employee creativity and productivity. The answer to this challenge lies in understanding employee motivation.

MOTIVATION

All human motivations are based on self-interest. We are motivated to do something only when it benefits us in some way. What about the common good? Are actions that support the common good also based on self-interest? Yes, but the self that has the interest is a different self. It is a self that transcends selfishness. It is a self with an enlarged sense of identity. It is a self that identifies with family, community, the organization it works for, society, and the planet. It is a self that recognizes that it is part of a web of interconnectedness that links all humanity and living systems. In management terminology, it is a self with a systems perspective. In spiritual terminology, it is a self that is in touch with its soul.

All human actions attempt to satisfy one of four needs—physical, emotional, mental, or spiritual. These needs correspond to nine basic human motivations. Our primary physical needs are met when we take care of our safety and health. Our basic emotional needs are met when we have strong personal relationships (friends and family) and feel good about ourselves (self-esteem). Our basic mental needs are fulfilled through educational or intellectual achievement and personal growth, and our spiritual needs are met when we find activities that give our life meaning and enable us to make a difference in the world by being of service to humanity or the planet. We find personal fulfillment when we are able to satisfy our physical, emotional, mental, and spiritual needs (see Figure 3–1).

Human Needs	Personal Motivation
Spiritual	9. Service
	8. Making a Difference
	7. Meaning
Mental	6. Personal Growth
	5. Achievement
Emotional	4. Self-Esteem
	3. Relationships
Physical	2. Health
	1. Safety

Figure 3–1
Relationship of Human Needs to Personal Motivation

There is a significant difference between the first five motivations and the last four. The first five serve the needs of ourselves as individuals. At these levels of motivation self-esteem is derived externally by what we own or possess, who we know, how smart we are, and being admired and respected by our friends, teachers, family, and colleagues.

Personal growth is satisfied not in the external world but in the internal world. Personal growth is a journey into self-knowledge that allows us to release our fears so that we can become all we can become. As we learn to understand our selves and our deepest motivations, we stop basing our self-esteem on what others think of us and start basing it on what we know of ourselves. This gives us the freedom to be who we really are, and it also gives us a greater sense of responsibility. We no longer blame others for our misfortunes. This new sense of personal responsibility demands that we question our old values and look for new values that will help us make better choices. This is the process of personal transformation.

As we make progress in personal transformation, we begin to recognize the importance of relationships. We are no longer interested in controlling others, but in supporting them in their development. As we learn to nurture and care for those around us, we develop an expanded sense of identity. Whatever we identify with we care for, because it becomes part of who we are. When we identify with our family, we care for their well-being. When we identify with our work unit and our organization, we care about their success. When we identify with our community and the planet, we become social and environmental stewards. We volunteer to help make the world a better place. We care about all these things because in this expanded sense of identity this is who we are. We feel the success and failures of those we care about as if they were our own.

The last three motivations—meaning, making a difference, and service—are based on the interest of the larger self—the one that identifies with our family, our work colleagues, our organization, our community, and the planet. The interests of this larger self are indistinguishable from the common good. Our lives take on meaning when we put our talents to use for this larger identity. When our efforts are appreciated and affect the world in a positive way, we feel that we have made a difference. When making a difference becomes the focus of our lives, we enter into the realm of service. At these higher levels of motivation our self-esteem is no longer derived externally through wealth, status, or beauty. It is derived internally through the contribution we make. I often ask people, why be content with happiness when you could have joy? Happiness springs from satisfying our physical, emotional, and mental needs. Joy springs from satisfying our spiritual needs—finding meaning, making a difference, and being of service. This is the most powerful human motivator. It unleashes depths of personal creativity and productivity that cannot be attained by purely external rewards. When we are able to satisfy our physical, emotional, mental, and spiritual needs, we are able to find personal fulfillment.

Productivity

When employees find personal fulfillment at work, the level of productivity can be at least twice as high as when they don't. A study of productivity found that for jobs of low, medium, and high complexity, highly motivated employees were respectively 52 percent, 85 percent, and 127 percent more productive than employees who had average motivation.[1] When the comparison was made between the most motivated and the least motivated employees, the level of productivity was 300 percent more for low-complexity jobs, 1200 percent more for medium-complexity jobs, and so large that it was unmeasurable for high-complexity jobs.

Another study involving 14 organizations and 25,000 employees found that approximately 39 percent of variability in corporate performance was attributed to the personal satisfaction of the employees based on a range of indicators that were a proxy for personal fulfillment. The same study found that 69 percent of the variability in personal satisfaction was attributable to the quality of the employees' relationship with their manager and their manager's empowerment skills.[2] This finding tends to confirm that emotional intelligence, which enables us to inspire and motivate others, is more important than intellectual intelligence in building a high-performance work force. Emotional intelligence not only allows us to bring out the best in others, it also allows us to become more productive and creative ourselves.

Personal Fulfillment

In *Creative Work*, Willis Harman and John Hormann discuss the relationship between meaning and creativity. They state "All of history supports the observation that the desire to create is a fundamental urge in humankind. Fundamentally we work to create, and only incidentally do we work to eat. That creativity may be in relationships, communication, service, art, or useful products. It comes close to being the central meaning of our lives."[3] The implication is that work without creativity has no meaning. If work is to be meaningful it *must* allow us to express our creativity. Without opportunities for expressing our creativity we are unlikely to find personal fulfillment.

Corporate America as a whole has not been successful at creating employee fulfillment and has not yet tapped the full potential of the American work force. According to a recent survey of more than 800 midcareer executives, unhappiness and dissatisfaction are at a 40-year high.[4] Four out of ten of those interviewed hated what they did. This proportion is double that surveyed four decades ago. When employees become this disenchanted with work, they are not prepared to go the extra mile because their hearts and souls are not in what they do. In such conditions they will not live up to their professional capacity. Either they are not being given work that is meaningful to them, or the organization's values are out of alignment with their personal values. Millions of people are no longer content with jobs and careers that satisfy only their physical, emotional, and mental needs. They want a work culture that aligns with their values and satisfies their spiritual needs too.

Job, Career, or Mission

We will be unable to find this satisfaction if we have the wrong attitude to work. There are three basic attitudes—work as a job, work as a career, and work as a mission.

Job.   A job is primarily about short-term security. We give time, energy, and skills to get money for survival and pleasure. A job fulfills our physical and emotional needs.

Career.   A career is primarily about long-term security. We give time, energy, skills, and knowledge to advance to higher levels of status and earning potential. We get comfort, security, and an opportunity to learn and grow. We also get a feeling of accomplishment. A career fulfills our physical, emotional, and mental needs.

Mission.   A mission is timeless. It is work that corresponds to our inner passion. We give our deepest selves. In return we find meaning. Our intuition and creativity come alive. When our work is also our mission and we have an employer who treats us fairly, we have an opportunity to find personal fulfillment.

In the twenty-first century, corporations will be building competitive advantage by nurturing creativity. This means they will be seeking ways to encourage every employee to have a mission mentality. Four conditions are necessary for this to happen:

1. Everyone in the organization must feel a powerful sense of connection to the "organizational identity." This requires a strong corporate culture with a shared vision and values that are in alignment with the employee's personal values.
2. The organization must (a) give everyone the opportunity to find work that corresponds to their inherent talents and passion and stretches them to become all they can become and (b) link the overarching mission of the organization to the individual mission of every employee.
3. The organization must create a culture and working conditions that allow employees to find personal fulfillment—to meet their physical, emotional, mental, and spiritual needs.
4. The organization must support employees in finding personal fulfillment by providing both professional and personal growth training.

We will discuss each of these topics in greater depth in subsequent chapters. For the moment, I would like to draw your attention to the important issue of institutionalizing creativity and making it an integral part of the corporate culture.

INNOVATE OR DIE

For many businesses, innovation and creativity are rapidly becoming a matter of economic survival. The link between economic survival and creativity is relatively new. It began with the industrial revolution. Up to the mid-nineteenth century, survival for the majority of the world's population was dependent on ownership of or access to land. Most people lived in rural areas and depended on land for their food and income. During the industrial revolution conditions for survival shifted from access to land for growing food to access to income for buying food. Thousands of people left agricultural jobs to work in factories. Competition for survival in the industrial economy was a matter of finding salaried work. Money became the asset that controlled survival. Initially, those who earned the most wages were those who could physically do the most work. Gradually, as the nature of work changed, knowledge replaced labor as the most valuable commodity. More importance was placed on education. Knowledge became the springboard for creativity and innovation. This was the new pathway to wealth.

World War II brought a major boost to creative activity. Faced with threats to physical survival a new spate of innovation was induced. This period spawned a host of new technologies such as radar, communications systems, the jet engine, and the harnessing of nuclear power.

During the two decades following the war, competition in the industrial economy was mostly national. Gradually, innovations in transportation and communications technologies enabled companies from different countries to compete with one another. By 1970 economic competition had become international; and by 1980 it had become global. Survival was no longer a local issue. Workers in the United States began competing for factory jobs with workers in Mexico. As economic rivalry stepped up to an international scale, new depths of creativity were unleashed. As a consequence, we have had more technological advancement in the past 50 years of Western civilization than in the whole of previous history.

French economist Georges Anderla of the Organization for Economic Cooperation and Development estimated in 1973 that humanity was doubling its knowledge every six years. He made this calculation assuming that the known scientific facts in A.D. 1 represented one unit of collective human knowledge. He calculated that it took until A.D. 1500 to double this knowledge. It doubled again in 1750, 1900, 1950, 1960, 1967, and 1973. More recently, Dr. Jacques Vallée has estimated that global knowledge is now doubling every 18 months.[5] As far as business is concerned, the exponential growth in knowledge provides inestimable opportunities for creating new products and building new businesses. The main limit to this expansion is the creative capacity of the work force. Increasingly, companies are finding that the creativity of their human capital is their key asset for expansion. Business guru Peter Drucker states: "Every organization needs one core competence: *innovation*." Richard Gurin, president and CEO of Binney & Smith, Inc. agrees with Drucker. "After a long business career, I have become increasingly concerned that the basic problem gripping the American workplace is the crisis of creativity." Walt Disney considered creativity to be so important that he paid his creative staff more than he paid himself.

Everyone Is Creative

The good news is that everyone is creative. It is a gift that we all possess, but many of us hide or lose it because it is socialized out of us at an early age or it is not appreciated by our employers. Dr. Calvin Taylor of the University of Utah found that all children are gifted and creative in some form. Some are creative in their speech, some in their body movements, and some in drawing and writing. Others are gifted in the way they relate to others or in the way they organize things.[6] The work of George Land and Beth Jarman reveals that the vast majority of children are creative geniuses. They gave the same group of 1,600 children a test of divergent creative thinking over a period of 15 years. From ages three to five, they found that 98 percent of the children scored in the genius category. At ages eight to ten, only 32 percent scored in that category. At ages 13 to 15, it was down to 10 percent. Two hundred thousand adults over the age of 25 have taken the same tests. Only 2 percent scored at the genius level.[7] What happened to their natural creativity? The answer is that it was socialized out of them. Our proficiency in expressing our creativity falls off as we accept other's opinions and evaluations of what is good and bad, right and wrong. Our education systems have much to answer in this arena. In the words of Jarman and Land, "That five-year-old creative genius is still lurking inside—just waiting to break free. It's not just in some of us, but it's in everyone."

The critical issue for business is how to mine that creativity. Thomas J. Watson, Jr., former IBM chief executive, highlights the importance of finding ways to bring out creativity in his 1963 booklet, *A Business and Its Beliefs*. He states, "I believe the real difference between success and failure in a corporation can be very often traced to the question of how well the organization brings out the great energies and talents of its people."[8] There are two critical elements in bringing out this creativity. The first is building a culture of employee participation and the second is institutionalizing the search for innovation.

Participation

The pathway to creativity begins with employee participation. There are five stages to participation—invitation, engagement, reflection, listening, and implementation. When an organization attempts participation for the first time, it needs to take care to complete all the steps. At the beginning, it is important to let *all* employees know that they are being invited to share their ideas and that their opinions are important. The engagement begins when employees are presented with information about the situation at hand and have the opportunity to ask questions. Reflection is necessary to allow them to digest the information and search for creative ideas. When employees come back with their ideas, management should engage in pure listening. When an organization attempts participation for the first time it may encounter pent up anger and cynicism. This is normal. When you take the lid off a boiling kettle, the steam will pour out.

If there is criticism of management, there should be no attempt to justify or defend past actions. If employees sense defensiveness on the part of those in authority or that they are not being heard, they will retreat into the "us" (the employees) and "them" (management) syndrome. Everyone's idea should be noted and acknowledged. Implementation should include as

many employee ideas as possible. The results should be communicated to all employees, and those whose ideas have been take
up should be congratulated and rewarded. When participation
becomes part of the corporate culture, employees feel that their
ideas matter and that management cares about what they think.
This engages their minds because they see their ideas can make a
difference. The workplace becomes a crucible for creativity and a
source of meaning that leads to a growing sense of commitment.

Commitment is enhanced when all those involved share a
common vision and values. Shared values build trust, and trust
gives employees responsible freedom. Responsible freedom
unlocks meaning and creativity. True power lies not in the ability
to control but in the ability to trust. People yearn for supervisors
who encourage them to explore their own creativity, because in
doing so the supervisor gives their life meaning.

In *The Empowered Manager*, Peter Block points out that in
every creative act there is a chance of failure: "Every act of creation is an act of faith. The essence of faith is to proceed without
any real evidence that our effort will be rewarded. The act of faith
in choosing to live out a way of operating that we alone believe in
gives real meaning to our work and our lives."[9] Because creativity involves uncertainty about outcomes, it is easily blocked by
fear. Most organizations fail to understand that for creativity to
flourish, employees must be given responsible freedom to express
themselves in their own unique way. They prevent creativity by
being overcontrolling and bureaucratic. In so doing they limit
their future survival. Creativity will not blossom in a rigid culture
that punishes failure. It requires a culture of trust that encourages
risk taking and in which both success and failure are celebrated.
Failure must be seen as a learning opportunity if creativity is to be
nurtured.

The traditional hierarchical model of management can prevent this from happening. In most organizations employees are
not paid to think—that is the prerogative of management—they
are paid to do. This quotation from a worker exemplifies the
issue: "For twenty years, you have paid for the work of my hands.
If you asked you could have had my mind for free." This culture,

which is prevalent in far too many organizations, prevents them from drawing on the wellspring of knowledge and creativity that employees are only too willing to share.

Traditional managers must learn to reinvent themselves. Managers who take on this challenge need to display four basic characteristics. The first, and for many the hardest part of the transformation, is that they must learn to be authentic. There must be no separation from who they are at home and who they are at work. They need to be able to bring their personal values to work if they are to become authentic individuals. Authenticity is a prerequisite for building trust. They must create an environment where everyone else can be themselves too. Second, managers must care about developing their people. The long-term interests of the company are best served when the employees are encouraged and given the opportunities to become all they can become. The more time spent in helping employees grow and develop, the more successful the organization will be. Third, managers must see their role as "barrier busters." They must eliminate roadblocks so that their teams can be fully productive and focus on what they do best.[10] Finally, managers must be a mentors and coaches to the employees who fall under their jurisdiction. Managers must shift their beliefs about their role from one of control and compliance to one of building motivation and commitment.

Institutionalizing Innovation

To build a truly creative culture, organizations must structurally integrate innovation into their operating processes and celebrate employees' creative ideas. In most high-innovation organizations a formal committee reporting to the management team is tasked with the responsibility of managing the search for innovative ideas. The committee should have sufficient stature and budget to set up cross-departmental project teams to support the exploration of the best ideas through feasibility studies. It should consider both process and product innovations. The committee should also be tasked with carrying out a critical review of the factors influencing the organization's market every year.[11]   It should therefore include not only internal and external technical specialists but also those who are knowledgeable about social, environmental, and economic trends. The committee should be culturally diverse, gender conscious, and include representatives from different age groups. It is vital in this process to make someone responsible for innovation and to measure innovation performance. In *Innovation Strategy for the Knowledge Economy*, Debra M. Amidon provides a short questionnaire for determining how well an organization is doing in institutionalizing innovation.[12] It includes questions such as:

- Has one person been chartered with the overall responsibility to managed the corporate-wide innovation process?
- Are there performance measures—both tangible and intangible—to assess the quality of your innovation practices?
- Is there a formal intelligence-gathering strategy to monitor the positioning of both current and potential competitors?
- Do your training/educational programs have provisions to incubate and spin out new products and businesses?

THE TWENTY-FIRST CENTURY ORGANIZATION

Successful organizations in the twenty-first century will be the ones that understand how to transform every job into a mission. They will be working with free-form flexible organizational structures that value participation and empower people to think. Without traditional hierarchies, academic qualifications will become less important. Emotional intelligence will become just as important as intellectual intelligence. People won't be promoted without both. The majority of new innovations will come from workers rather than managers. The manager's and supervisor's main role will be to set up the conditions that nurture creativity—a working environment that supports the physical, emotional, mental, and spiritual well-being of workers (see Figure 3–2).

Organizations of the future will compete for the best employees by providing health and medical facilities for them and their families, kindergartens for their children, and social

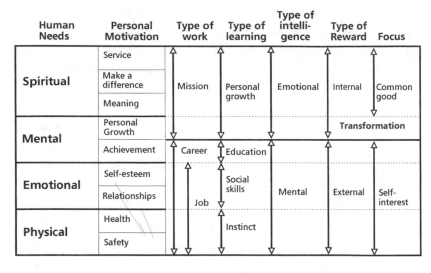

Human Needs	Personal Motivation	Type of work	Type of learning	Type of intelligence	Type of Reward	Focus
Spiritual	Service Make a difference Meaning	Mission	Personal growth	Emotional	Internal	Common good
Mental	Personal Growth				Transformation	
	Achievement	Career	Education			
Emotional	Self-esteem Relationships	Job	Social skills	Mental	External	Self-interest
Physical	Health Safety		Instinct			

Figure 3–2
Relationship of Personal Motivation to Type of Work, Type of Learning,
Type of Intelligence, Type of Reward, and Focus

workers and chaplains to support their emotional and spiritual
needs. Some will even go so far as to hire people to do urgent
errands and chores for employees. Companies that are already
experimenting with these services have shown that they bring
high rates of return. Marriott International created a Family
Resource Line that connects Marriott employees to a multilingual
staff of social workers who help them address their problems.
During a seven-month period, 17,000 Marriott workers made use
of this facility. Preliminary surveys showed that Marriott was getting a 418 percent rate of return on its investment in terms of
reduced absenteeism, better quality work, and improved relationships with co-workers. One employee survey found that 29 percent of workers who used the service would otherwise have quit
their jobs because they were overwhelmed by their problems.[13]

A recent survey reported in *Fortune* magazine[14] found that
the 100 Best Companies in America are finding inventive ways to
retain their employees. At least 39 of these companies, including
General Mills, Johnson & Johnson, Intel, and Xerox, will do your

dry cleaning, and many others, such as AlliedSignal, Honda of America, and Starbucks, offer personal concierge services. With unemployment in America at a 25-year low, companies are desperate to hold on to their employees. Many companies have learned the hard way that downsizing can severely hurt their ability to compete. They lost so many talented people during reengineering that they are frantically rehiring.

Why does this quality of care matter? Because the energy that people spend worrying about personal issues or dealing with emergencies detracts from their ability to focus their minds on their work. When people are worried, overly stressed, or fearful about their futures or their families, their creativity and productivity decrease. Visionary organizations see their employees as having a range of needs. They understand that caring for the total well-being of their workers produces a competitive advantage in the form of a committed and motivated work force.

Successful organizations in the twenty-first century will have cultures very different from those of the twentieth century. They will pursue a broad range of goals that support the physical, mental, emotional, and spiritual health of their employees. They will create a working environment that nurtures participation, innovation, and creativity. Senior managers will be tasked with making innovation part of the structural framework of the organization. Successful organizations in the twenty-first century will encourage employees to develop their natural talents and to follow their mission. They will become trusted members of the local community and good global citizens. They will be doing all these things because this is what it will take to attract the most talented people and achieve long-lasting financial success.

Notes

1. Michael Cox and Michael E. Rock, *Seven Pillars of Leadership* (Toronto: Dryden, 1997), pp. 10–13.
2. Study of Business Performance, Employee Satisfaction, and Leadership, Wilson Learning Corporation.

3. Willis Harman and John Hormann, *Creative Work* (Indianapolis: Institute of Noetic Sciences, 1990), p. 26.

4. Article in the *Washington Post*, August 25, 1996, by Richard Merlin reporting on a survey by Joy Schneer of Rider University and Frieda Reitman of Pace University.

5. Peter Russell, *The White Hole in Time* (San Francisco: Harper, 1992), p. 28.

6. George Land and Beth Jarman, *Breaking Point and Beyond* (San Francisco: HarperBusiness, 1993), p. 153.

7. Ibid.

8. James C. Collins and Jerry I. Porras, *Built to Last: Successful Habits of Visionary Companies* (New York: HarperCollins, 1994), p. 73.

9. Peter Block, *The Empowered Manager* (San Francisco: Jossey-Bass, 1987), p. 195.

10. For a discussion of the role of managers, see *Managing in the High Commitment Workplace* by Kim Fisher, Self-Managed Teams (New York: American Management Association, 1994), pp. 27–41.

11. For a discussion on innovation practices, see Managerial Practices That Enhance Innovation, by Andre L. Delbecq and Peter K. Mills, *The Creative Edge* (New York: American Management Association, 1994), pp. 39–47.

12. Debra M. Amidon, *Innovation Strategy for the Knowledge Economy: The Ken Awakening* (Boston: Butterworth-Heinemann, 1997), pp. 62–63.

13. *Washington Post*, October 1, 1995, Workplace by Kirstin Downay Grimsley.

14. Anne Fisher, The 100 Best Companies to Work for in America, *Fortune* Magazine, January 1998, pp. 69–70.

4

Seven Levels of Organizational Consciousness

When we align our thoughts, emotions and actions with the highest part of ourselves, we are filled with enthusiasm, purpose and meaning.

—GARY ZUKAV

With the emergence of self-reflective consciousness the platform of evolution moved up from life to consciousness. Consciousness became the spearhead of evolution. Conscious inner evolution is the particular phase of evolution that we are currently passing through.

—PETER RUSSELL, *THE GLOBAL BRAIN*

Just as, long ago, self-consciousness appeared in the best specimens of our ancestoral race in the prime of their life, and gradually became more and more universal and appeared in the individual at an earlier and earlier age, . . . so will cosmic consciousness become more and more universal and appear earlier in the individual life until the race at large will possess this faculty.

—RICHARD MAURICE BUCKE, *COSMIC CONSCIOUSNESS*

The previous chapter discussed the relationship between the four categories of human needs and the nine personal motivations. This chapter consolidates the nine personal motivations into Seven Levels of Human Consciousness, from which we will develop Seven Levels of Employee Consciousness and Seven Levels of Organizational Consciousness.*

A FRAMEWORK OF HUMAN CONSCIOUSNESS

The Lower Levels of Consciousness

The first four of the Seven Levels of Human Consciousness correspond closely to Abraham Maslow's hierarchy of human needs—security, relationship, self-esteem, and self-actualization. Our physical needs are satisfied when we feel secure. Our emotional needs are met when we establish meaningful relationships with others and feel good about ourselves. Self-knowledge and personal mastery help us satisfy our mental needs.

Survival Consciousness
The most important category of human needs is survival. We need clean air, food, and water to keep our bodies alive and healthy. We also need to keep ourselves safe from harm and injury. Our basic motivation at this level of consciousness is self-preservation. Whenever we feel threatened or insecure physically or economically, we shift into "survival" consciousness. In most situations the fear generated is a healthy fear. Fear forces us to focus on our physical and economic well-being. When an individual becomes overly fearful or has deep insecurities, survival consciousness can become a way of life. Such individuals easily get angry. The source of their anger is a nagging feeling that nobody cares about them. Whenever something goes wrong they see it as a personal threat. They believe they live in a hostile environment. They are constantly on guard and feel that if they don't

---

* Consciousness: A state of awareness of self (thoughts, feelings, ideas) based on a set of beliefs and values through which reality is interpreted. A shift to a higher state of consciousness involves a change in beliefs, values, and behaviors. The values at the higher level of consciousness promote greater inclusiveness and connectedness and less separation and fragmentation.

look out for themselves no one else will. Consequently, to feel safe they feel they must control everything around them. They have great difficulty in trusting.

Relationship Consciousness

The second category of human needs is relationship. We satisfy this need when we develop meaningful attachments to those with whom we share a common identity. Belonging is important to us because we are by nature social creatures. The ability to communicate openly and honestly helps us establish such relationships. When individual have fears about being liked or included, relationship consciousness can become a way of life. Such individuals are constantly looking for signs of inclusion or affection. In this state of consciousness it is easy to develop dysfunctional codependent relationships. When the need for relationship is strong, individuals will do things against their own better judgment to prove that they are worthy of being part of the group. In some cases individuals are prepared to suffer abuse to be in relationship with others.

Self-Esteem Consciousness

The third category of human needs is self-esteem. We satisfy this need when we feel respected by those with whom we share a common identity. Gaining the respect of others gives us a sense of our own self-worth. When an individual has deep-seated fears about self-worth, self-esteem consciousness can become a way of life. In such situations, individuals seek to assuage their need for self-esteem through status, wealth, or beauty. They become overly ambitious or competitive. They want to stand out and be noticed, particularly by those with whom they share a common identity. They may even attempt to persuade themselves how good they are by becoming arrogant. Their greatest fear is that they are not valued or respected.

Our physical and emotional needs are satisfied in the external world. We seek money for security, we develop relationships to feel a sense of belonging, and we attempt to gain the respect of others to bolster our self-esteem. When we are centered in the three lower levels of consciousness we live in a state of object referral. Our sense of who we are is to a large extent dependent on the opinions we believe others hold of us. The greater our fears, the more deeply we are attached to these opinions. To break the grip of these fears we need to shift from a state of object-referral to a state of self-referral.

Self-Actualization

We achieve a state of self-referral when we release the fears that cause our insecurities. In this state we no longer care what we believe others think of us. We care more about what we think of ourselves. As we become independent of others opinions, we become more responsible for our selves. Rather than reacting to a situation from our unconscious fears, we can now choose how to respond. We shift from a state of *react*-ability to a state of *response*-ability. We achieve this state through personal transformation—self-knowledge and personal growth. This is the state that Maslow referred to as self-actualization. Self-actualized individuals seek answers to questions such as, Who am I? Why am I here? and How can I become a better person?

Maslow described self-actualization as "A state in which a person becomes more ego-transcending and more independent of the lower needs."[1] During self-actualization we become less controlled by the fears that drive our lower needs. We develop the ability to see that our real self-interest is intimately entwined with the interest of the common good. This is called "enlightened" self-interest. The "enlightenment" has to do with the ability to perceive and understand ourselves as forming part of the pattern of interconnectedness of life—what modern management literature calls the systems perspective.

Maslow described self-actualized individuals in the following way: "Self-actualizing people are, without one single exception, involved in a cause outside of themselves. They are devoted, working at something which is very precious to them—some calling or vocation. They are working at something that fate has called them to somehow and which they work at and which they love, so that the work-joy dichotomy in them disappears."[2]

Maslow's studies led him to the conclusion that self-actualized individuals are motivated by spiritual needs. He summarized his findings in the following way: "The hierarchy of basic needs is prepotent to the meta-needs (self-transcendent needs). What all this means is that the so-called spiritual life is on the same continuum with the life of the body. The spiritual life is part of our biological life. It is the highest part of it."[3] Although Maslow did not delineate the higher states of consciousness, he did identify the values that self-actualized individuals integrate into their lives. These values include truth, goodness, unity, wholeness, uniqueness, aliveness, perfection, justice, order, richness, simplicity, playfulness, self-sufficiency, and meaningfulness. He called these values the ultimate values.

The Higher Levels of Consciousness

To get a clearer idea of the needs and motivations of the higher or spiritual states of the consciousness, we must turn to Vedic science.[4] Charles Alexander and Robert Boyer of the Department of Psychology at the Mahahrishi International University in Fairfield, Iowa, describe four levels of spiritual consciousness. Each level corresponds to an increasingly enlarged sense of personal identity brought about by a greater sense of connectedness to the world.

Soul Consciousness

The first level is soul consciousness. This corresponds very closely to the state that Maslow calls self-actualization and Roberto Assagioli, the Italian psychotherapist, calls psychosynthesis.[5] In this state of consciousness the separation between the ego and the soul disappears as we release the fears concerning our physical and emotional needs. We let go of how we think we should be and become who we really are. Swiss psychiatrist Carl Jung called this process individuation—the integration of the unconscious content of our minds into our conscious awareness. In other words, bringing our unconscious fears into our conscious awareness. By so doing we learn to master our fears and increase our *response*-ability. As we move through this process our personality becomes less fragmented and more whole. We become more authentic in our relationships and find clarity around our purpose. Fulfilling that purpose becomes one of our strongest motivations.

Cosmic Consciousness

The next level is cosmic consciousness. It is a permanent state of soul consciousness in which the personality and the soul become indistinguishable. In this state, individuals are able to achieve their full potential. We encounter and integrate our authentic selves. We want to work on our mission 24 hours a day. Life becomes infused with meaning. Creativity and intuition are abundant. Connection to our family, our community, and our work colleagues becomes vital because it is through and with them that we are able to fulfill our potential and give our lives meaning. We begin to develop an enlarged sense of identity and recognize that our self-interest is wrapped up in the good of the whole.

Divine Consciousness

Beyond cosmic consciousness lies divine consciousness. In this state of consciousness the individual experiences a strong connectedness to the whole of creation. We begin to identify with the humanity and the planet. The beauty of the Earth and its flora and fauna are fully appreciated and the interdependence of all life forms is recognized. At this level we are no longer content with meaningful work, we want our work to make a real difference in the world. We need to know that we are making a positive contribution. We seek partnerships to increase our effectiveness. If we cannot make a contribution through our formal work, then we seek to become a community volunteer and social and/or environmental steward.

Unity Consciousness

The last stage is unity consciousness. In this state there is no separation between the knower and the object of knowing. The self fuses with the self aspect of all creation. We become one with all there is. We seek to be of service by making a difference in everything that we do. We recognize that what we do for others we are doing for ourselves. We want our work to affect the whole of

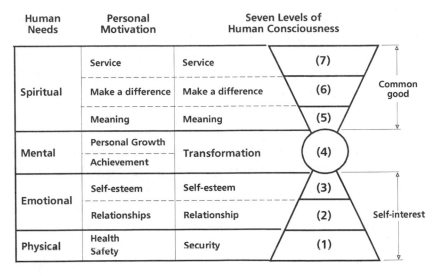

Figure 4–1
Relationship of Human Needs and Personal Motivation to the Seven
Levels of Human Consciousness

society. We become concerned with the global situation. Our life
becomes a life of service to humanity and the planet.

The higher levels of consciousness are dominated by love
and feelings of connectedness. The lower levels of consciousness
tend to be dominated by fear. This fear is experienced as a sense
of separation and fragmentation.

I have consolidated the nine personal motivations and the
eight levels of consciousness described above into seven levels of
human consciousness. Health and safety motivations have been
combined under the category security, and personal achievement
and growth have been combined under the category of transformation. The resulting seven levels of human consciousness are
shown in Figure 4–1.

SEVEN LEVELS OF EMPLOYEE CONSCIOUSNESS

Understanding the seven levels of human consciousness has
important implications for business. Organizations that do not
support transformation, or give employees opportunities to find

meaning through their work, to make a difference and be of service to the world, are severely limiting their potential for success. Not only are they failing to access the intuition and creativity of their employees, they are forgoing the opportunity to build the emotional intelligence of their managers. As seen in Figure 3–2, emotional intelligence is an attribute of those who focus on personal growth and satisfy their spiritual needs. Companies that understand the importance of the seven levels of human consciousness not only allow employees to design their own personal and professional training programs but also provide time off for employees to work in the local community. They recognize the importance of satisfying employees' physical, emotional, mental, and spiritual needs. The seven levels of human consciousness translate directly into seven levels of employee consciousness.

1. Survival Consciousness

The first basic need of employees is financial security. Everyone who works wants to know that their job is secure and that they can look forward to a regular paycheck. It is about this issue that employees suffer their greatest fears. When employees are too entrenched in this level of consciousness, they become preoccupied with money and feel insecure about their future. This can lead to an obsessive need to control or to know what is going on. Employees at this level of consciousness can spend an excessive amount of time gossiping. They can also be very cautious and fearful about making decisions. They find it difficult to delegate. They tend to believe that the world is an intrinsically hostile place and find it difficult to trust. Consequently, they become exceedingly territorial and see life as a series of battles to get what they want. They fear change because they regard the unknown as a threat. Fear of survival is manifest as a lack of trust.

2. Relationship Consciousness

The second basic need of employees is to find friendship and camaraderie among colleagues. When employees are too entrenched in this level of consciousness, their need for relationship is driven by fear. This is called codependency. Codependency is motivated by *getting* from others what *you* need to allay *your* insecurities. Community is motivated by *giving* to others what *they* need to allay *their* insecurities. The emotional needs of the codependent worker can be so great that they are willing to do anything to feel part of the team. Their codependency demands that they sacrifice their desires and suppress their feelings so as not to endanger their membership of the group. Consequently, they will find it difficult to speak their minds in situations in which there are divergent views. They sacrifice truth and their creativity for the security of belonging. They would rather stay silent than risk upsetting anyone. They are concerned about their image because they want to be liked. They fear change because of the impact it may have on their carefully constructed emotional support systems. In this state of consciousness, loyalty to one's colleagues is more important than loyalty to the company.

3. Self-Esteem Consciousness

The third basic need of employees is to gain respect. They want to feel good about themselves. Employees who operate from this level of consciousness care about improving their salary and/or position. When their need for self-esteem is very strong they can become ambitious and competitive. They will lie or tell half-truths rather than give their superior bad news. They live in a state of object-referral in which their feelings of self-worth are derived externally. Their focus is on getting what they need to look good. The greatest fear of those who live in self-esteem consciousness is that they are not respected and appreciated. They are searching for approval, and they will try to get it in any way they can. If it means working long hours or traveling continuously, they will do it. They lack balance in their lives and are willing to sacrifice their family, their friends, and their colleagues for the sake of their work. They need to be the best, the most highly paid, and they are most certainly hankering after access to the executive dining room. Termination or early retirement can be devastating for these people. So much of their identity is wrapped up in work that they don't know who they really are. They fear change because of the impact it may have on their status. If you know an individual who operates from levels of self-esteem *and* survival consciousness, watch your back. If you are in the way, a knife may appear in it.

4. Transformation Consciousness

Individuals enter self-actualization when they become so uncomfortable with certain aspects of their lives that they are prepared to reexamine their beliefs. The situation that sparks this introspection may be a devastating event in their personal lives or a challenging experience at work or a series of upsets that cause profound reflection. The process of transformation begins when an individual takes full responsibility for the way things are. Only when they stop blaming others for their misfortunes and pain can they see reality objectively. During transformation, there is a shift from unconscious reaction to conscious choice—from living in fear to living in truth. As people make these changes, they let go of their need to control and begin to trust. During self-actualization the individual enters into a struggle for understanding, a search for meaning, and a deep-felt need for truth. This quest for truth centers around two questions: "Who am I?" and "Why am I here?" They find answers to these questions as they develop their personal vision and mission. They become aware of the importance of values to guide them in their daily decision making. As they discover their deeper motivations, they search for ways to express who they really are.

5. Organization Consciousness

The principal focus for employees at this level of consciousness is the search for meaning through work. They no longer think in terms of job or career but see work as a way to give meaning to their lives. Employees who operate from this level of consciousness are constantly seeking ways in which they can improve their effectiveness. They see their self-interest as best served by supporting the good of the whole. They recognize the importance of sharing and networking. They have a strong sense of values and actively seek to express them through their work. They are constantly seeking to learn and grow. They are intuitive and creative. They are not afraid to be vulnerable and can be counted on to express their opinions and feelings with honesty. They recognize the importance of sound relationships and are good at interpersonal skills. Consequently, they have a strong sense of integrity and work well in teams. At this level of consciousness, employees are able to clarify and deepen their personal vision and bring a sense of play and fun to their work.

6. Community Consciousness

The principal focus for employees at this level of consciousness is making a difference in the world. They have an enlarged sense of responsibility that embraces not only the workplace but the local community as well. They care very strongly about the company and the community because both are part of their identity. They are particularly concerned about environmental and social issues. They are stewards of the planet and have a humanitarian outlook. At this level of consciousness, employees become highly intuitive and creative. They see their organization and their work as a vehicle to fulfill their mission and goals. They do not pay significant attention to rewards. They are focused on personal fulfillment. They are not defensive and are easily accessible. They are willing to go the extra mile, provided they can keep their lives in balance. Individuals at this level of consciousness maintain an internal state of detachment that allows them to access their full mental potential in all situations.

7. Society Consciousness

The principal focus of employees at this level of consciousness is service. They have a world outlook and keep abreast of international developments. They are aware of the major issues facing society and are active in finding solutions. They are very concerned about ethics. Society-conscious individuals are respected and trusted, and their opinions are frequently sought. They see the world as a complex web of interconnectedness. Every aspect of their lives is meaningful. Everything they do is with purpose. They can be given free reign. They will do what is ethically and morally correct. Their constant preoccupations are how to support the good of the whole and make sure the organization has a beneficial impact on the world. They are visionary in their approach—always anticipating what is required or necessary. They are patient while others catch up with their ideas. Periods of solitude and meditation are essential for their well-being. Because of the nature of their insights, they are often not well understood. They are intuitive and creative. What they have to say and give to the world is extremely important. The inner life of these individuals includes deep silence, unshakable commitment, and a frequent sense of joy and contentment.

Distribution of Consciousness
It is rare to find individuals exclusively focused at one particular level of consciousness. Most frequently people display characteristics associated with three or four adjacent levels. The center of emphasis tends to be either in the lower three levels of consciousness (self-interest), in the upper three levels (the common good), or around transformation. During times of stress, such as takeovers or downsizing, the center of emphasis tends to shift to the lower three levels of consciousness. Fear for one's survival can significantly change the distribution of employee consciousness.

SEVEN LEVELS OF CORPORATE CONSCIOUSNESS

A fundamental thesis of this book is that organizations are living entities that share motivations similar to those of individuals. Every organization has a distinct personality, which is called the corporate culture. The corporate culture is built around a set of complex beliefs and assumptions that make up a mental model of how people in the company believe the world ought to be. In start-up companies the corporate culture corresponds to the personality of the founder. When the founder hands over authority to a CEO, the culture begins to take on some of the aspects of the personality of the new leader. As a company grows in size it

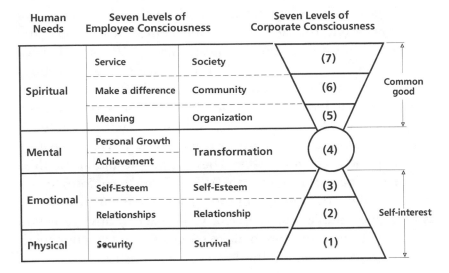

Human Needs	Seven Levels of Employee Consciousness		Seven Levels of Corporate Consciousness		
Spiritual	Service	Society	(7)		Common good
	Make a difference	Community	(6)		
	Meaning	Organization	(5)		
Mental	Personal Growth / Achievement	Transformation	(4)		
Emotional	Self-Esteem	Self-Esteem	(3)		Self-interest
	Relationships	Relationship	(2)		
Physical	Security	Survival	(1)		

Figure 4–2
Relationship of the Seven Levels of Employee Consciousness to the Seven Levels of Corporate Consciousness

begins to develop its own culture, but only to the degree that the CEO and founder allow. If the company is to achieve long-lasting success it must develop a culture that is independent of the personality of the leader. It must establish a culture and an identity of its own based on the collective motivations and shared values of all the people who work in the company. When this happens, a core culture emerges that supports the common good. The organization becomes a living entity with a distinct personality. Self-interest of the individuals in the organization becomes aligned with the good of the whole. The different stages of this evolution can be summarized in Seven Levels of Corporate Consciousness. The relationship of the Seven Levels of Employee Consciousness to the Seven Levels of Corporate Consciousness is shown in Figure 4–2.

1. Survival Consciousness
The first need for an organization is financial survival. Without profits or access to a continuing stream of funds, organizations

quickly perish. Every organization needs to make financial health a primary concern. However, when companies become too entrenched in survival consciousness, they develop an exclusive preoccupation with the bottom line and a deep-seated insecurity about the future. They attempt to allay their fears through excessive control and territorial behavior. Businesses that operate from this level of consciousness are not interested in strategic alliances—takeovers are more their game. They will purchase a company and plunder its assets. They see people and the Earth as resources to be exploited for gain. When asked to conform to regulations, they do the minimum. They have an attitude of begrudging compliance. They feel victimized by any regulation that restricts their freedom to make money. Organizations experience their deepest fears at this level of consciousness.

2. Relationship Consciousness

The second need for an organization is harmonious interpersonal relationships. Without good relationships with employees, customers, and suppliers, company survival is compromised. Companies deeply entrenched in this level of consciousness place importance on relationships not for what they can give, but for what they can take. They look at relationships purely from the perspective of having their needs met. What they put into a relationship is purely based on what they think they will get back. Companies at this level are strong on tradition and image and weak on flexibility and entrepreneurship. Rules are important because there is little trust. They demand discipline and obedience from their employees. Family businesses tend to operate from relationship consciousness. They limit their ability to become successful because they are unable to trust outsiders in management positions. To grow and develop, family-run businesses must shift to a higher level of consciousness.

3. Self-Esteem Consciousness

The third need for an organization is self-esteem. Self-esteem consciousness shows up in organizations as a desire for greatness. Organizations that operate from this level want to be the biggest or best at what they do. Consequently, they are very competitive and are constantly seeking ways to improve their cost-effectiveness. Organizations at this level see management as a science. They focus on improving corporate fitness—productivity, efficiency, time management, and quality control. They are ready to train their staff as long as the training has a direct impact on the bottom line. Control is maintained through hierarchical power structures that often do little more than cater to the managers' needs for status, privilege, and recognition. Companies that are predominantly focused at this level of consciousness can easily degenerate into bureaucracies. When this happens, failure or collapse will eventually occur unless the organization is able to embrace transformation.

4. Transformation Consciousness

This is the bridge that companies must cross if they are to create organizational cohesion and shift their belief systems from self-interest to the common good. The principal focus at this level of consciousness is self-knowledge and renewal. Organizations enter the process of transformation either because it is the next natural step in their evolution or because their viability is threatened. In either case, the process begins with employee participation and involvement. Everyone is asked to take responsibility for making the business a success. During transformation, the culture of the organization shifts from control to trust, from punishment to incentives, from exploitation to ownership, and from fear to truth. Mechanisms are put in place to promote innovation and learning. The tyranny of the financial bottom line begins to disappear as organizations start to measure their success against a broad set of indicators. Vision, mission, and values are recognized as the means to develop a strong core identity and internal cohesion.

5. Organization Consciousness

The primary focus of organizations at this level of consciousness is internal connectedness. They achieve this through the development of a positive culture that supports employee fulfillment. By focusing on the needs of its people, the organization encourages higher levels of personal productivity and creativity. This occurs as a natural by-product of building trust, community spirit, and internal cohesion. Values such as transparency and equality become important. Risk taking is encouraged. Failures become lessons and work becomes fun. At this level of consciousness, organizations recognize the importance of people finding meaning and purpose through their work. They encourage the alignment of their employees' personal motivations with the organization's vision and mission and support employees in becoming all they can become in terms of their professional and personal growth.

6. Community Consciousness

The primary focus of organizations at this level is external connectedness. They achieve this by creating partnerships with customers and suppliers and supporting the local community. Organizations that embrace community consciousness recognize the importance of strategic alliances and being respected members of the community and good global citizens. They seek to support the local economy by collaborating with local businesses and voluntarily carrying out environmental and social audits. They go beyond the letter of the law in dealing with their responsibilities. They support employees in finding personal fulfillment at work and create opportunities for them to make a difference in the local community. At this level of consciousness organizations care for the whole employee—for their physical, emotional, mental, and spiritual needs.

7. Society Consciousness

The primary focus of organizations at this level of consciousness is service to humanity and the planet. There is a recognition of the interconnectedness of all life and the need for both individuals and institutions to take responsibility for the welfare of the whole. At this level of consciousness organizations care deeply about ethics, justice, human rights, peace, and the impact of present day actions on future generations—sustainable development. Social activism and consciously directed philanthropy become integral parts of their corporate strategy. They understand the importance of societal goodwill in building a successful organization. They observe the highest ethical principles and always consider the long-term impacts of their decisions and actions. By taking a strong moral position, they are able to garner the respect and goodwill of their employees and society at large.

Distribution of Consciousness
Organizations rarely operate from a single level of consciousness. They tend to cluster around three or four levels. Most organizations in America are strongly focused in the lower three levels of consciousness—profit (level 1), customer satisfaction (level 2), and productivity (level 3). The organizations that make the list of the 100 Best Companies in America tend to focus on upper levels of consciousness—innovation (level 4), employee fulfillment (level 5), and customer and supplier collaboration (level 6). They also find ways to care for the local community (level 6) and make a contribution to society (level 7).

This type of distribution of consciousness is known in Japan as kyosei (creating a spirit of cooperation in which the individual and the organization work together for the common good). After the kyosei culture was introduced into Canon, it became the world market-share leader in copiers and desktop printers. The company's profits grew at an annual rate of 20 percent. Sales grew at 9 percent per annum, and the return on equity more than doubled.[6] In Canon the spirit of the common good has become an operating reality. However, it did not happen overnight. The company had first to become financially viable. Once it became profitable, it had the resources to make *kyosei* work. Without profit it is difficult to make a significant contribution to the common good.

Notes

1. Abraham H. Maslow, *The Farther Reaches of Human Nature* (New York: Penguin Books, 1976).
2. Ibid., p. 42.

3. Abraham H. Maslow, *Toward a Psychology of Being* (New York: Van Nostrand Reinhold, 1968).

4. "Seven States of Consciousness," Charles N. Alexander and Robert W. Boyer, *Modern Science and Vedic Science*, Vol. 2, No. 4, pp. 325–364, 1989, Department of Psychology, Mahahrishi International University, Fairfield, Iowa.

5. Roberto Assagioli, *Psychosynthesis: A Manual of Principles and Techniques* (Wellingborough: Crucible, 1990).

6. Ryuzaburo Kaku, "The path of Kyosei," *Harvard Business Review*, July–August 1997, pp. 55–63.

5

Corporate Transformation Tools

If a corporation is to develop or manage its culture, to achieve its mission, it is absolutely essential to know what values it currently has.

—Brian Hall, *Values Shift*

Measurement matters: If you can't measure it, you can't manage it.

—Robert S. Kaplan, David P. Norton, *The Balanced Scorecard*

While most companies provide for people's basic provisions, we contend that it's essential to create an environment in which higher-level needs are satisfied.

—Hal F. Rosenbluth, CEO of Rosenbluth Travel

THE TOOLS

Based on the framework of the Seven Levels of Corporate Consciousness, I have developed a series of survey instruments to support organizations in building cultural capital, strengthening human resource capacity, developing values-based leadership and promoting socially and environmentally sustainable development. Collectively, these instruments are called Corporate Transformation Tools[SM]. For more information contact www.corptools.com. The tools can be used for the following purposes:

- Corporate and team culture assessment
- Leadership values assessment
- Employee exit assessment

- Employee entry assessment
- Client assessment of corporate values
- Mergers and acquisition cultural compatibility assessment

1. Corporate and Team Culture Assessment

The corporate value audit instrument consists of three templates of values/behaviors from which individuals in an organization can choose the ten values that most represent who they are (personal values), the ten values that best describe how their organization/team operates (organizational values), and the ten values they believe are essential for a high-performance organization/team (ideal organizational values). Each value/behavior on the three templates is associated with one of the seven levels of corporate consciousness, is either positive or potentially limiting (negative), and is categorized as either a personal value (e.g. integrity), a team value (e.g. trust), an organizational value (e.g. customer satisfaction), or a societal value (e.g. environmental protection).

The templates of values/behaviors are customized for each organization and its operating environment. The customization consists of adding or subtracting values/behaviors to or from a standard values template in three stages: (a) adding values that are included in the organization's vision, mission, and values statements; (b) adding values that relate to the sector of activity and predominant professional disciplines (retail, manufacturing, media, education, banking, medical, etc.) and removing those that do not; and (c) adding values/behaviors that are particular to the national culture and language.

The results of the organization's value audit can be disaggregated horizontally by group, such as the management team, middle managers, and staff; vertically by department, such as operations, sales, administration, or by factory or store location; and by demographic factors such as gender, length of service, age, and race.

The corporate values audit instrument is used as a diagnostic tool to evaluate the strengths and weaknesses of existing corporate or team cultures. Case studies in the use of the values audit instrument appear later in this chapter. This instrument:

- Identifies the top ten personal, organizational, and ideal organizational values for the whole organization and by group and department, including demographic differences.
- Assesses the degree of alignment between the top ten personal values, the top ten organizational values, and the top ten ideal values.
- Identifies the distribution of personal values, organizational values, and ideal organizational values according to the seven levels of organizational consciousness.
- Indicates the degree to which the organization's culture is focused on self-interest, transformation, and the common good.
- Indicates the degree of alignment between the organization's actual values and its espoused values.
- Identifies the behavioral changes that are necessary to build a long-lasting successful organizational culture.
- Identifies the organization's positive and limiting values and the ratio of personal, team, organizational, and societal values.
- Measures the degree of consensus around the top ten personal values, organizational values, and ideal organizational values.

2. Leadership Values Assessment

This instrument provides 360 degree personal feedback to help executives develop their leadership skills. It uses templates of values/behaviors. One is used by the individual to describe his or her personal style. The other is used by assessors. The results of the self-assessment and the feedback assessments are compared (see Chapter 10). The Leadership Values Assessment:

- Compares the distribution of the individual's perception of his or her own organizational values with the perception of his or her colleagues according to the seven levels of leadership consciousness (see Chapter 9)

- Compares the individual's perception of his or her own top ten organizational values with the perception of his or her colleagues
- Indicates the degree to which the individual's values are focused on self-interest, transformation, and the common good
- Identifies the degree of alignment between the individual's operating values and the organization's espoused values
- Identifies the behavioral changes that the individual needs to make to grow as a leader
- Identifies the individual's limiting values and the ratio of the individual's personal, team, organizational, and societal values
- Identifies the type of leadership development program that is appropriate for the individual

3. Employee Exit Assessment

This instrument provides feedback from exiting employees on their perception of the corporate culture. It consists of three templates of values/behaviors—Personal Values, Organizational Values and Ideal Organizational Values. The results can be disaggregated into voluntary leavers, retirees, and forced leavers. The instrument provides information on:

- Exiting employees' perceptions of the corporate culture according to the seven levels of organizational consciousness
- The degree of alignment between exiting employees personal values and their perception of the organization's values
- The degree of alignment between exiting employees ideal organizational values and their perception of the organization's values

- The exiting employees' perception of the degree of alignment between the organization's actual values and espoused values
- The exiting employees' perception of the organization's positive and limiting values

4. Employee Entry Assessment

Once a successful corporate culture has been introduced, it is important to maintain the culture by selecting employees that have similar operating values. This instrument provides feedback on the compatibility of potential employees' organizational values with the organization's espoused values. It consists of two templates—the employee's perception of his or her operational values and the employee's perception of ideal organizational values. The instrument provides information on:

- The alignment of employees' operating values with the company's ideal employee values profile
- The alignment of potential employees' ideal organizational values with the organization's espoused values

5. Client Assessment of Corporate Values

Visionary organizations frequently assess their performance based on client feedback. The client assessment instrument can be used to access the perceptions of customer, suppliers, and society-at-large. The values/behavior templates are customized to reflect the organization's espoused values, professional discipline, and sector of activity. The instrument can be used to:

- Identify client perceptions of the organization's operating values
- Compare client's perceptions of the organization with employee's perceptions
- Compare client's perceptions with the organization's espoused values

Cultural Indices

Five cultural indices can be derived from the values audit instruments.

CTS Index: Measures the percentage of values voted for by a particular group that are situated in the upper three levels of consciousness (Common good), the middle level (Transformation), and the lower three levels of consciousness (Self-interest). Positive high-performing cultures tend to have more than half their values situated in the upper levels of consciousness and a significant proportion of the remainder at the transformation level.

PL Index: Measures the proportion of the top ten values that are *Positive* and those that are potentially *Limiting*. An index of 10–0 or 9–1 can be regarded as highly positive. An index of 7–3 or worse can be regarded as negative or highly limiting.

PTOS Index: Measures the ratio of *Personal, Team, Organizational,* and *Societal* values in the group's top ten organizational and ideal organizational values. The personal values assessment does not contain any *Organizational* values. Therefore it has a **PTS** Index. The **PTOS (P)** includes only positive values. The **PTOS (L)** includes only limiting values. The distribution of personal, team, organizational, and societal values is an important cultural indicator. High-performing organizational cultures tend to have a strong foundation of personal and team values, with some organizational values and at least one societal value, for example, 4–3–2–1 or 3–4–2–1 (see Figure 5–1).

ST Index: Measures the *ST*rength of the culture. The index represents the percentage of votes received by the top ten values compared with the total number of votes cast by individuals in a particular group.

BNS Index: This index measures the distribution of the top ten organizational or ideal organizational values to a six-part Balanced Needs Scorecard. The categories used in the score-

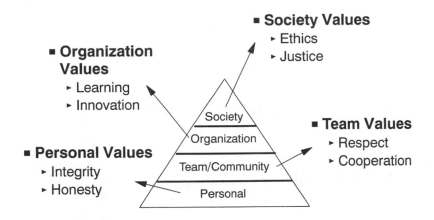

Figure 5–1
Corporate Values Pyramid: Strong Organizational Cultures Are Built on
a Firm Foundation of Personal and Team Values

card are Corporate Survival, Corporate Fitness, Customer
and Supplier Relations, Corporate Evolution, Corporate
Culture, and Societal and Community Contribution. The use
of this index is described in Chapter 7.

CASE STUDIES: CORPORATE VALUES AUDIT

The following case studies provide examples of the use of the values audit instrument.

Company A

Company A is in plastics. It has 1,000 employees and was established in 1955. Its mission statement includes values such as
growth, superior products, strategic alliances, innovation, creativity, customer care, open honest communication, teamwork,
quality, continuous improvement, profit, and return to shareholders. No attempt has been made to communicate these values
to managers or employees. The company has five factories. Three
of them have been recently assimilated into the company by
acquisition. Three of the five factories make products that are very

Company A: Management

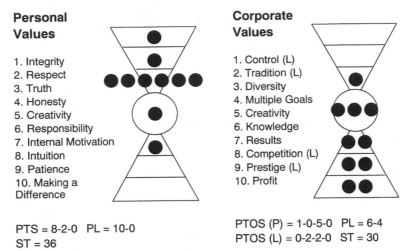

Personal Values

1. Integrity
2. Respect
3. Truth
4. Honesty
5. Creativity
6. Responsibility
7. Internal Motivation
8. Intuition
9. Patience
10. Making a Difference

PTS = 8-2-0 PL = 10-0
ST = 36

Corporate Values

1. Control (L)
2. Tradition (L)
3. Diversity
4. Multiple Goals
5. Creativity
6. Knowledge
7. Results
8. Competition (L)
9. Prestige (L)
10. Profit

PTOS (P) = 1-0-5-0 PL = 6-4
PTOS (L) = 0-2-2-0 ST = 30

Figure 5-2
Company A: Top Ten Personal and Organizational Values of the Management Team (Each dot represents one of the top ten values.)

Company A: Management

Personal Values   CTS = 51-21-28
Corporate Values CTS = 37-20-43

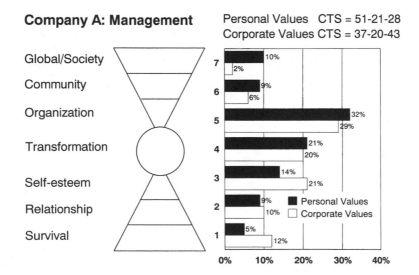

Global/Society
Community
Organization
Transformation
Self-esteem
Relationship
Survival

7 — 10% / 2%
6 — 9% / 6%
5 — 32% / 29%
4 — 21% / 20%
3 — 14% / 21%
2 — 9% / 10%
1 — 5% / 12%

■ Personal Values
☐ Corporate Values

0%   10%   20%   30%   40%

Figure 5-3
Company A: Distribution of Personal and Organizational Values of the Management Team

Company A: Factory Staff

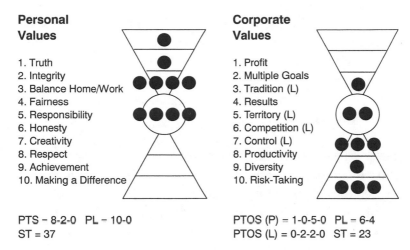

Personal Values

1. Truth
2. Integrity
3. Balance Home/Work
4. Fairness
5. Responsibility
6. Honesty
7. Creativity
8. Respect
9. Achievement
10. Making a Difference

PTS – 8-2-0   PL – 10-0
ST = 37

Corporate Values

1. Profit
2. Multiple Goals
3. Tradition (L)
4. Results
5. Territory (L)
6. Competition (L)
7. Control (L)
8. Productivity
9. Diversity
10. Risk-Taking

PTOS (P) = 1-0-5-0   PL – 6-4
PTOS (L) = 0-2-2-0   ST = 23

Figure 5–4

Company A: Top Ten Personal and Organizational Values of the Factory Staff (Each dot represents one of the top ten values.)

Company A: Factory Staff

Personal Values   CTS = 50-24-26
Corporate Values CTS = 41-14-45

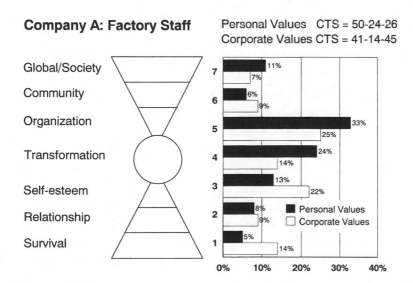

Global/Society — 7 — 11% / 7%
Community — 6 — 6% / 9%
Organization — 5 — 33% / 25%
Transformation — 4 — 24% / 14%
Self-esteem — 3 — 13% / 22%
Relationship — 2 — 8% / 9%
Survival — 1 — 5% / 14%

■ Personal Values
□ Corporate Values

0%   10%   20%   30%   40%

Figure 5–5

Company A: Distribution of Personal and Organizational Values of the Factory Staff similar. The company is struggling to make profits. Training is heavily focused on skills.

The values audit instrument was used to assess the personal and corporate values of the ten-member corporate management team and a group of employees from the principal factory. The management team comprises the president, the head of corporate marketing, the chief financial officer, the head of research, and the managers of the five factories.

Company A: Results of the Values Audit

A cursory examination of the results shows an immediate disparity between the distribution of personal and organizational values across the seven levels of consciousness for management and staff. The CTS indices for both groups are very similar. They have personal value cultures 51–21–28 (management) and 50–24–26 (staff) that focus on the common good and corporate value cultures 37–20–43 (management) and 41–14–45 (staff) that focus on self-interest. Clearly, there is very little alignment between personal and corporate values in this organization. This is usually indicative of a dysfunctional organizational culture.

The top ten organizational values of the management team and factory staff help us to identify the exact nature of this dysfunction. Both groups identify four limiting values—control, tradition, competition, and prestige in the case of the management team and control, tradition, competition, and territory in the case of the staff. Notice that three of the limiting values in both groups are the same (see Figures 5–2 and 5–3). Control blocks trust, tradition can prevent entrepreneurship, internal competition prevents cohesion, prestige focuses on form rather than results, and territory prevents cooperation.

A measure of the dysfunction of the management team is the fact that control was recognized as the number one cultural behavior. The management team's core culture also includes competition. This is reflected in competition in the marketplace between factory managers. The management team placed profit as number ten on their list of cultural values, whereas staff recognized it as the most important value. Customer care, quality, strategic alliances, and employee involvement did not make it into the organization's top ten values. Out of the 12 values espoused by the organization in its mission statement, only three showed up in the top ten values of managers and staff—profit, productivity, and creativity.

Management and staff were also in close agreement on the PTOS index. Both groups scored high on organizational values and low on personal and team values. The PTOS (P) for management was 1–0–5–0 and the PTOS (L) was 0–2–2–0. The PTOS (P) for staff was 1–0–5–0 and the PTOS (L) was 0–2–2–0. The team values chosen by both groups were all limiting values. Creativity (management) and risk-taking (staff) were the only positive personal values. Neither group recognized any societal values in the core culture. The PTOS index shows that the existing organizational culture is low in positive personal and team values, indicating very little trust and cohesion. This conclusion is supported by the CTS indices, which show a greater emphasis on self-interest than the common good.

A ray of hope for this organization is that the ST (strength) index of the existing culture is weak. A weak negative culture is easier to transform than a strong negative culture. The top ten values of the management team represented only 30 percent of the total votes cast. The top ten values of the staff represented only 23 percent of the votes cast. Part of the reason for the weakness of the culture is the lack of a shared vision, mission, and values.

The distribution of values also sends a message of hope. The greatest proportion of values voted for by managers and staff was in level 5—the level of organizational cohesion (see Figures 5–3 and 5–5). Despite this strong showing, the only value from this level to make it into manager's top ten was creativity and the staff's top ten was risk-taking.

The results of the values audit for Company A point to three major areas of improvement:

- The need to build a culture of trust and collaboration among the management team
- The need to define a common vision and shared values

- The need for more employee involvement and greater customer focus

It was recognized by all concerned that the first order of priority was to address the dysfunctionalities of the management team. The management team had to be able model team-based behaviors (a shift from control to trust and from competition to cooperation) before the organizational transformation could proceed. The Leadership Values Assessment, which is described in Chapter 10, was used to highlight each member of the management team's leadership challenges and suggest appropriate leadership development programs. The second order of priority was to define a common vision and shared values. It was decided that this would be done only after the issues in the management team had been resolved.

Case Study: Company B

Company B is in travel services. It has 12 employees and was established in 1986. The company has a mission statement that has been shared with all employees. It includes the following values: participation, trust, wealth, teamwork, compassion, and social and environmental awareness. The company consistently makes profits, of which 15 percent are donated to good causes. The company pays for employees to follow both personal and professional studies of their own choosing.

Company B: Results of Values Audit

A quick examination of Figure 5–6 and 5–7 shows a close alignment between the distribution of the staff's top ten personal and top ten organizational values. The CTS indices, which measure the overall distribution of values, are also close for the personal and organizational values, 60–22–18 (personal) and 53–29–18 (organizational). In both cases the majority of values lie in the upper levels of consciousness—a focus on the common good. We can conclude that the staff in Company B find a high degree of personal fulfillment. Employee fulfillment and physical, emotional, mental,

Company B: All Staff

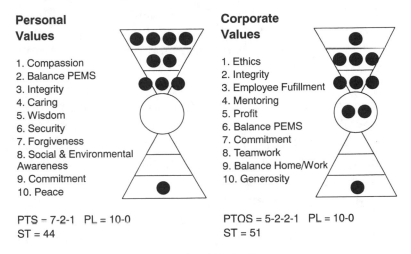

Personal Values

1. Compassion
2. Balance PEMS
3. Integrity
4. Caring
5. Wisdom
6. Security
7. Forgiveness
8. Social & Environmental Awareness
9. Commitment
10. Peace

PTS = 7-2-1   PL = 10-0
ST = 44

Corporate Values

1. Ethics
2. Integrity
3. Employee Fufillment
4. Mentoring
5. Profit
6. Balance PEMS
7. Commitment
8. Teamwork
9. Balance Home/Work
10. Generosity

PTOS = 5-2-2-1   PL = 10-0
ST = 51

PEMS = Physical, Mental, Emotonal and Spiritual

Figure 5–6
Company B: Top Ten Personal and Organizational Values of All Staff

Company: All Staff

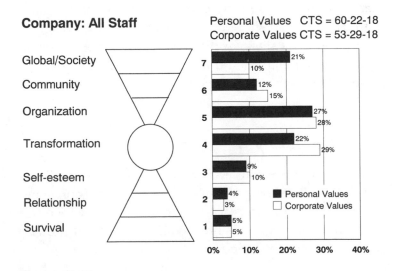

Personal Values   CTS = 60-22-18
Corporate Values CTS = 53-29-18

Global/Society — 7 — 21% / 10%
Community — 6 — 12% / 15%
Organization — 5 — 27% / 28%
Transformation — 4 — 22% / 29%
Self-esteem — 3 — 9% / 10%
Relationship — 2 — 4% / 3%
Survival — 1 — 5% / 5%

■ Personal Values
□ Corporate Values

0%   10%   20%   30%   40%

Figure 5–7
Company B: Distribution of Personal and Organizational Values of All Staff

and spiritual fulfillment (Balance PEMS) are both included in the organization's top ten values. The organization has no limiting values. One of the dangers that Company B faces is in becoming too altruistically focused. It is reassuring, therefore, to see profit showing up as one of its top ten values.

The PTOS index, 5–2–2–1, shows a strong foundation of personal values with two team values (mentoring and teamwork), two organizational values (employee fulfillment and profit), and one societal value (ethics). The organizational ST index of 51 indicates a strong core culture. Company B is clearly living up to the values expressed in its mission statement.

Despite Company B's strong positive values, there are some troubling aspects of its culture. The lack of level 3 values suggests that order, systems, and productivity may be a problem, and the lack of values regarding customer care also raises some concerns. Company B has one major client. It renegotiates this contract every two years. As a result of the values audit, Company B revised its values statement to give greater focus to customer orientation and produced a brochure to attract new clients.

The purpose of the first two case studies was (a) to illustrate the significance of the relationship between personal and organizational values and (b) to show how important it is to disaggregate the organization's values for different levels of the organization. The purpose of the third and fourth case studies is to show the important role that the ideal organizational values can play in the values audit.

Case Study: Company C

Company C is a large newspaper. It has 250 employees and was established in 1962. The company does not have a mission statement. Ten years ago it put in place a diversity policy, which has been actively pursued. Figure 5–8 presents the results of the values audit of the top 40 managers.

The most striking feature of the Company C values audit is the lack of alignment between the existing organizational values and the personal and ideal organizational values. The existing

Company C: Top 40 Managers

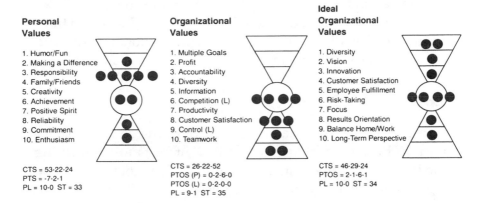

Personal Values	Organizational Values	Ideal Organizational Values
1. Humor/Fun	1. Multiple Goals	1. Diversity
2. Making a Difference	2. Profit	2. Vision
3. Responsibility	3. Accountability	3. Innovation
4. Family/Friends	4. Diversity	4. Customer Satisfaction
5. Creativity	5. Information	5. Employee Fulfillment
6. Achievement	6. Competition (L)	6. Risk-Taking
7. Positive Spirit	7. Productivity	7. Focus
8. Reliability	8. Customer Satisfaction	8. Results Orientation
9. Commitment	9. Control (L)	9. Balance Home/Work
10. Enthusiasm	10. Teamwork	10. Long-Term Perspective

CTS = 53-22-24
PTS = -7-2-1
PL = 10-0   ST = 33

CTS = 26-22-52
PTOS (P) = 0-2-6-0
PTOS (L) = 0-2-0-0
PL = 9-1   ST = 35

CTS = 46-29-24
PTOS = 2-1-6-1
PL = 10-0   ST = 34

Figure 5-8
Company C: Top Ten Personal, Organizational, and Ideal Organizational Values of Managers

organizational CTS index is strongly focused on self-interest (26–22–52). The personal CTS index (53–22–24) and the ideal organizational CTS index (46–29–24) are strongly focused on the common good. There are no personal values in the existing organization's PTOS (P) 0–2–6–0, and two of the team values are limiting (control and competition) PTOS (L) 0–2–0–0. None of the top ten values are located at the level of organizational cohesion (level 5). The lack of personal values and the limiting team values, together with the strong focus on self-interest, create a very stressful work environment.

The ideal organizational values support Company C's diversity policy but also call for greater sense of vision and long-term perspective. The managers also want to see a greater emphasis on home/work balance and employee fulfillment. The strong "T" value in the ideal organizational CTS index (29) is calling for more employee involvement and greater innovation, creativity, and risk-taking.

The positive aspects of Company C's existing culture are its focus on diversity, accountability, profit, productivity, and customer satisfaction. The challenge it faces is to shift from being primarily a level 3 organization with some level 1, 2, and 4 attributes to becoming a level 5 organization with some level 1, 2, 3, and 4 attributes. This shift from level 3 to level 5 involves transformation. The distribution of ideal organizational values suggests that the managers are ready to take on this challenge.

Case Study: Company D

Company D is an small, family-owned U.S. conglomerate that has been in business for 70 years. It has interests in engineering, media, and food processing. The company does not have a vision, mission, or values statement. Two years before the values audit the company invited an outsider to become the CEO. It also began renewing its senior staff with younger, more professionally orientated managers. Figure 5–9 presents the results of a values audit of the top 30 managers.

The most striking feature of the values audit is the lack of consistency between the manager's personal, organizational, and ideal organizational values. Vision and honesty are the only values that appear twice. Vision appears in the personal and ideal organizational lists, and honesty appears in the personal and organizational lists.

The list of personal values is consistent with a group of young professionals who are focused on personal success and achievement. The PTS index has 8 personal values, 2 team values, and no societal values. The list of organization values reflects a more mature outlook that engenders community spirit, PTOS (P) 3–4–0–1. It has 3 positive personal values, 4 positive team values, no organizational values, and 1 societal value. The top ten organizational values contain two limiting values—tradition and caution, PTOS (L) 1–0–1–0. These two values headed the list of organizational values. The list of ideal organizational values reflects a "let's get organized" outlook, PTOS (P)1–1–6–1, PTOS (L) 0–1–0–0. This list, which is headed by productivity and vision, contains 1 personal value, 1 positive and 1 limiting team value, 6 organizational values, and no societal values.

Company D: Top 30 Managers

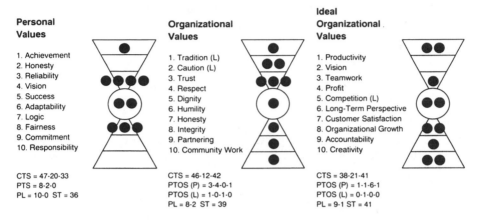

Personal Values	Organizational Values	Ideal Organizational Values
1. Achievement	1. Tradition (L)	1. Productivity
2. Honesty	2. Caution (L)	2. Vision
3. Reliability	3. Trust	3. Teamwork
4. Vision	4. Respect	4. Profit
5. Success	5. Dignity	5. Competition (L)
6. Adaptability	6. Humility	6. Long-Term Perspective
7. Logic	7. Honesty	7. Customer Satisfaction
8. Fairness	8. Integrity	8. Organizational Growth
9. Commitment	9. Partnering	9. Accountability
10. Responsibility	10. Community Work	10. Creativity

CTS = 47-20-33	CTS = 46-12-42	CTS = 38-21-41
PTS = 8-2-0	PTOS (P) = 3-4-0-1	PTOS (P) = 1-1-6-1
PL = 10-0 ST = 36	PTOS (L) = 1-0-1-0	PTOS (L) = 0-1-0-0
	PL = 8-2 ST = 39	PL = 9-1 ST = 41

Figure 5–9

Company D: Top Ten Personal, Organizational, and Ideal Organizational Values of Managers

Another striking feature of the values audit is the difference between the organizational and ideal organizational CTS indices. The ideal organizational CTS index shows more emphasis on self-interest, 38–21–41, than the existing organizational CTS index, 46–12–42. This is because the focus of the family directors has always been on personal relationships and doing the right thing. The company is operating from a values-driven but very tradition-oriented level 2 consciousness and has not been able to make a transition to level 3—productivity, order, efficiency—or level 4—employee participation, learning, teamwork. A very positive level 2 consciousness often has personal values that are similar to those of level 5 organizations. It is important to note that the "T" component of the CTS index of the existing culture is very low (12). This indicates a low tolerance for innovation, learning, and employee participation. The desired "T" value in the ideal organizational values is 21. There is a clear message here that the young managers want more involvement in the running of the company. They see the old culture, based on strong family values, as cautious and lacking in entrepreneurial spirit. They want the company to be more focused on profit and growth (level 1); on customer satisfaction (level 2); on productivity and competition (level 3); on teamwork, accountability, and employee participation (level 4); and on creativity (level 5). The challenge that the family-run board of directors faces is to open up the decision-making processes to professional managers and at the same time retain the level 5 values of trust, integrity, and honesty so that the company can preserve a sense of community and organizational cohesion.

These examples of the use of the values audit instrument raise several questions:

- How does the values audit relate to the use and sequencing of other corporate transformation tools?
- Can the results of the values audit be used to assess an organization's readiness for cultural transformation?
- Is there an ideal values distribution that is applicable to all organizations?

Sequencing of the Use of Corporate Transformation Tools^{SM}

The sequencing of the use of the Corporate Transformation Tools^{SM} is important. It is essential to start with the values audit in order to (a) highlight the existing cultural issues and (b) establish baseline indicators. Down the line, the success of the cultural transformation process can be assessed by carrying out further values audits and comparing the results with the baseline measures.

Successful cultural transformation programs begin with the modeling of the espoused values and behaviors by the management team. That is why it is important to assess the values of this group separately from the organization as a whole. There will always be some differences between the values of the management team and the rest of the organization, but as we saw in the case of Company A, the key cultural issues of the management team are often reflected in the organization as a whole. Very often the source of the dysfunctionality may lie in the values/behaviors of the president or CEO.

If the results of the culture assessment show strong dysfunctionality at the level of the management team, it will be important to carry out a Leadership Values Assessment before progressing with the implementation of a cultural transformation program. If the values audit does not bring to light any significant issues in the management team, then the next step would be to proceed with the definition of the corporate mission, vision, and values (see Chapter 6) and establish a Balanced Needs Scorecard (see Chapter 7).

A detailed overview of a framework and process of cultural transformation is fully described in Chapter 11, Building a Visionary Organization.

Assessing an Organization's Readiness for Cultural Transformation

It is important to recognize the difference between *need* and *readiness* for cultural transformation. Many organizations need to transform their cultures, but they may not be ready. Success depends on achieving a state of readiness. Readiness depends on two factors: (a) the commitment of the leader and the management team to their own personal transformation and (b) a cultural predisposition to transformation throughout the organization. Organizational transformation will not occur unless the management team is able to walk the new talk, and organizational transformation will not be easy to implement if the organization does not have values and behaviors that promote internal cohesion such as trust, integrity, openness, and transparency.

The CTS index is a good indicator to assess readiness for transformation both at the level of the management team and at the level of the organization as a whole. Readiness for transformation occurs when there is a strong "T" component in the CTS index or a reasonably strong showing of values at the level of organizational consciousness (level 5).

In the case study of Company A the "T" component of the CTS index for the management team had a reasonably strong value of 20 and the proportion of values at the level of organizational consciousness was high—28. The "T" value for staff was 14, but the proportion of values at the level of organizational consciousness was high—25. This shows that there is a reasonably strong cultural predisposition to transformation. If the control, tradition, competition, and prestige issues can be overcome in the management team, it is likely that a successful transformation can be accomplished.

Company B is in a higher state of readiness for transformation than Company A. The "T" value for Company B is 29 and the proportion of values at level 5 was 28. In Company B, 57 percent of the corporate values were located at levels 4 and 5. Company B has moved beyond the state of cultural transformation and is now embarked on cultural evolution—a continuous state of corporate transformation.

Company C has a strong "T" value (22) and an even stronger ideal organizational "T" value (29). The managers in Company C have an appetite for transformation. Although Company D has a low existing "T" value, 12, it has a strong latent desire for transformation. The managers' ideal organizational "T" value is 21.

The Ideal Culture

The answer to the question "Is there an ideal values distribution that is applicable to all organizations?" is, "It depends." There are certain values that are found in almost all successful organizations, and there are other values that depend on the type of activity and the predominant professional culture. The values that are found in most successful organizations relate to profit or income, effective communications and personal relationships, productivity, quality and results orientation, participation, learning and innovation, trust, openness, diversity and creativity, strategic alliances, customer and supplier collaboration, community and society contribution, and vision. Let us call these the core values for success.

Activity-Based Values

The values that are activity based tend to relate to the specifics of the work that the organization performs. For example, the values for an ideal university department, an ideal religious institution, an ideal military unit, and an ideal sports team would be different.[1] The university department would focus on achievement (external learning). This could be called a competence culture. The military unit would focus on discipline. This could be called a control culture. The religious institution would focus on personal growth (personal development). This could be called a cultivation culture; and the sports team would focus on teamwork. This could be called a collaboration culture.[2] For each of these different types of organizations to be successful, they would also need to display the core values for success listed before.

Profession-Based Values

Because of their training, executives, engineers, and operators (those who are involved in actual production rather than manage, supervise, or plan) not only use different languages but also bring different sets of assumptions to their work.[3] The operating assumptions of executives and engineers tend to be based on their worldwide occupational community rather than on their organization's values. Financial and managerial executives often focus on order, information, and profit. Engineers tend to focus on systems, knowledge, and productivity.

Edgar Schein, Professor of Management at the MIT Sloan School of Management, believes that executives and engineers tend to "see people as impersonal resources that generate problems rather than solutions . . . they view people and relationships as means to the end of efficiency and productivity, not as ends in themselves."[4] The operator culture, on the other hand, tends to focus on what works—values such as participation, teamwork, and collaboration—in other words, values that align with getting the job done and organizational cohesion.

Society-Based Values

In addition to activity- and profession-based values, multinational organizations also need to take account of the cultural values of the countries in which their factories or offices are located. They should be very wary about exporting North American-based values to other parts of the world. For example, values that pertain to gender equality or sexual orientation that for the most part may be acceptable in North America may be less acceptable in Europe or the Middle East.

The research is very clear on this topic—people in different countries value different things. Sirota and Greenwood[5] investigated the work goals of 19,000 employees in a large multinational electrical equipment manufacturer operating in 46 countries. They found that Northern European countries expressed less interest in "getting ahead" and work recognition goals and put more emphasis on job accomplishment; in addition, they showed more concern for people and less for the organization as a whole. English-speaking countries tend to value individual achievement more than security. French countries gave greater importance to security and somewhat less to challenging work. Latin countries and especially southern Europeans, were less concerned about individual achievement and more concerned about job security. Fringe benefits were important to Latin countries. Germans valued security, fringe benefits, and getting ahead. Japanese were less concerned about advancement and autonomy but very concerned about challenge. They also had a strong emphasis on good working conditions and a friendly working environment.

Although research supports the idea that basic human needs are similar, they highlight that culture and environment play an important role in ordering these needs[6] and determining how they can best be met. Hence, it is quite possible for a multinational company to have a shared core culture as long as it is sensitive to societal differences and sets up incentive and reward structures that are tailored to individual countries. Based on extensive research on the *International Dimensions of Organizational Behavior*, Nancy Adler concludes that, "Organizations world-wide are growing more similar, while behavior of people within organizations is maintaining its cultural uniqueness."[7]

The Composite Picture

From the foregoing, I conclude that there is a core culture that leads to organizational success but that in any given situation this culture may be modified by three factors:

- Activity-determined values
- Professional values
- Cultural or societal values

The challenge for leaders is to build an organizational culture that maximizes the development of human potential and strategic alliances while working within the framework of acceptable values and behaviors that relate to the type of activity, the dominant professional discipline, and the mores of the local community. We will explore the leadership qualities necessary to accomplish such a task in Chapters 9 and 10.

MERGERS AND TAKEOVERS

Another important use of the values audit instrument is in assessing the cultural compatibility and integration issues of organizations that are involved in mergers or takeovers. A survey of more than 300 big mergers over the past ten years by Mercer Management Consulting, based in New York, found that in the three years following these transactions, 57 percent of the merged firms lagged behind their industries in terms of their total returns to shareholders.[8] The long-run failure rate of mergers appears to be even higher. The main reasons for merger disappointment are the lack of an integration strategy and failure to appreciate the difficulties of blending together two different corporate cultures. Fusing the formal systems, such as accounts, payroll, and financial reporting, has its difficulties, but these can pale in comparison with the problem of the integration of cultures.

Mergers that occur between companies with similar values and levels of organizational consciousness have the greatest chance of being successful. The next most successful are those that involve higher level cultures taking over lower level cultures. In such situations the benefits of shifting to a higher level culture will be attractive to most employees but may cause consternation to managers who operate from the lower levels of consciousness and find it difficult to come to terms with employee participation. With coaching, training, and personal growth seminars, some managers may be able to shift to the higher culture. Others will never make it and will eventually leave. The least successful takeovers are those that involve companies that operate from the lower levels of consciousness taking over companies that operate from the higher levels of consciousness.

A notable example was the take over of Celestial Seasonings by Kraft in 1984. Up to that point in time, the culture of Celestial Seasonings had been one of equality and family spirit. Kraft brought in hierarchy and reserved parking spaces. They also wanted all employees to undergo drug testing. This was unacceptable to the management of Celestial and eventually led to an expensive divorce.[9] Quaker also suffered a culture problem when they took over Snapple, a soft drinks maker with a laid-back and idiosyncratic management style. The employees of Snapple were alienated by Quaker's attempts to change Snapple's culture.[10] The 1993 union of Price Club and Costco Wholesale, two discount retailers, was in disarray in less than a year after their merger, due largely to the vastly different management cultures.[11]

"Due diligence" on an organization's culture is rarely considered in mergers and acquisitions and yet it is likely to be the most important factor for a successful outcome. Unfortunately, most businesses are so stuck in self-esteem (being the biggest or best) and survival consciousness (profitability) issues when they are considering mergers that they tend to overlook personality differences. They enter into the arrangement as if they were a marriage partner intent on dominating or using the other person for their own ends. Such an attitude quickly turns marriages sour. When you fail to consider the "feelings" of your partner, disaster quickly follows. I use the word "feelings" without caution, because *that* is the issue in a large number of failed mergers—the feelings of the management and staff of the company being taken over are not considered or respected. When one company culture is allowed to take over another, it often means that the very culture that led to the need for the merger is allowed to perpetuate. Without a change in culture, the problem that may have led to the need for a merger may remain.[12]

Southwest Airlines, a company that operates from a higher state of consciousness, did due diligence on the culture of Morris Air when they merged with them in 1993. It looked at everything, from Morris' systems and schedules to its entrepreneurial culture. The result—a successful and profitable takeover.[13] When Federal Express, another higher consciousness organization, took over Flying Tigers, they invited Tiger employees and their wives to Memphis to see if they wanted to relocate. They were welcomed with a red carpet and dozens of Federal Express employees cheering them on. Everyone in Flying Tigers was offered a job.[14]

The key issue in takeovers and mergers is the same as in marriage—how will the two personalities get along? Arranged marriages can be just as successful as "love" marriages, if the two personalities are similar or complement one another. A marriage between partners will work only if there is mutual respect and neither of the partners precipitously attempts to change the personality of the other. McKinsey has found that successful acquirers value continuity of management. In successful takeovers 85 percent of buyers left their target's managers in place.

The merger of the U.K.-based Beecham Group with the U.S.-based SmithKline Beckman overcame the problems of attempting to merge cultures by creating a new culture. What began as a merger of equals became a complete transformation.[15] The first stage involved changing the management team of the Beecham group and defining a new strategy for growth. In stage two the companies created a single structure. Stage three involved defining a new set of values and behaviors in alignment with the growth strategy. A new culture was born. This led to stage four—the creation of a new management architecture that supported the achievement of the strategic goals of the new culture. In 1986 the Beecham Group ranked twenty-third in world pharmaceuticals and SmithKline Beckman ranked ninth. By 1994 the joint firm, SmithKline Beecham, ranked fifth in world pharmaceuticals and second in health care. Revenues from continuing operations grew 40 percent in less than five years and pretax profits increased by more than 75 percent.

REENGINEERING AND DOWNSIZING

As we discussed earlier, reengineering is a tool for change. It is not a tool for transformation. Change typically involves incremental improvements in efficiency, cost-effectiveness, or productivity and is seen by organizations that operate from the lower levels of corporate consciousness as a panacea for success. At best, reengineering improves corporate fitness; at worst, it undermines morale and destroys the social fabric of the organization. The reason why so few reengineering initiatives have been successful is that they failed to take into account the human factors of change. The real challenge of reengineering is how to introduce systems improvements without losing the loyalty and commitment of the work force. The answer lies in the way that reengineering is approached. Organizations that operate from the higher levels of consciousness tackle reengineering differently from those that operate from the lower levels of consciousness. At the lower levels, little attention is paid to the human and psychological factors. Consequently, the process is painful. Consultants are called in, plans are drawn up, and employees are displaced as rapidly as possible. The process is efficient but uncaring. Any gains in productivity and efficiency are compromised by the slump in morale, motivation, and commitment.

In companies that operate from higher levels of consciousness, reengineering involves a considerable amount of staff participation and a great deal of communication. Those who work in the departments to be reengineered, and are ready to embrace change, are placed in charge of the studies. If layoffs are required, they are handled with compassion. Inducements are offered to those who would like to take early retirement, and retraining or outplacement services are offered to others.

When it comes to layoffs, people and processes are very important to organizations that operate from the higher states of consciousness. When Knight-Ridder had to lay off staff, they were open and honest with everyone. They began by cutting at the top. All officers' salaries were frozen for 18 months. All those below officer level had their salary frozen for 15 months. Most of the people whose positions were eliminated were given other jobs in the company, and outplacement services were provided for the small number who did leave.

When Federal Express shut down its Zapmail program in 1986, all 1,300 employees were given priority on its internal job postings. Employees who could not find positions with equivalent salaries could take lower level jobs and retain their previous salary for up to 15 months or until they found a higher salary job.[16] Federal Express's CEO, Fred Smith, operates a "people first" policy that is described in the company's *Manager's Guide* as: "Take care of our people, they in turn, will deliver impeccable service demanded by our customers who will reward us with the profitability necessary to secure our future. People–Service–Profit, these words are the very foundation of Federal Express."[17]

In *The 100 Best Companies to Work for in America*, Levering and Moskowitz list 17 companies that have implicit no-layoff policies and have been through difficult periods without resorting to layoffs. In addition to Federal Express, the list includes companies such as Hallmark Cards, Northwestern Mutual Life, Hewitt Associates, Southwest Airlines, and H. B. Fuller.

H. B. Fuller is a leading maker of adhesives, sealants, and coatings. Fuller has never laid off its employees since it began operating in 1887. In the event of a work stoppage, employees are still guaranteed at least 32 hours of work a week. If there's not enough to do in the plant, employees are paid to do community work. Fuller promises all employees that if their job becomes obsolete they will be retrained in a new technology. Like Fuller, Hallmark is one of the few companies in the United States that has yet to lay off employees. In the early 1980s, 600 employees were reshuffled around to other jobs because there was not enough production work to keep them busy. Some had their salaries paid while they did community work.

Hewitt Associates, the fourth largest consultant in the design of compensation and benefit programs for companies, also maintains a no-layoff policy. That policy was severely tested in 1991 during a downturn in business. Everyone was informed of the acute financial situation and asked to pitch in with cost saving ideas. Austerity measures were instituted that included canceling the company picnic and cutting down on flowers in the office. People were told to expect lower or no pay raises, with the burden falling mainly on the senior associates. Expenses were cut by $15 million a year and no one had to be laid off.

Companies that operate with values that support the common good are able to maintain morale, commitment, and loyalty even during difficult times. When staff reductions are necessary because of a downturn in sales, companies that operate from the higher levels of consciousness explore ways to share the burden. If this doesn't work, layoffs are handled with compassion and caring.

Notes

1. William E. Schneider, *The Reengineering Alternative: A Plan for Making Your Current Culture Work* (Chicago: Richard D. Irwin, Inc.),1994, p.11.

2. Ibid., p. 103.

3. Edgar H. Schein, "Three cultures of management: The key to organizational learning," *Sloan Management Review,* Fall 1996, pp. 9–20.

4. Ibid., p. 16.

5. D. Sirota and M. J. Greenwood, "Understanding your overseas work-force," *Harvard Business Review,* Vol 14, January–February 1971, pp. 53–60. Quoted in Nancy J. Adler, *International Dimensions of Organizational Behavior* (Belmont: Wadsworth Publishing Company, 1991), p. 158.

6. Nancy J. Adler, *International Dimensions of Organizational Behavior* (Belmont: Wadsworth Publishing Company, 1991), p. 154.

7. Ibid., p. 57.

8. "Why so many mergers miss the mark," *The Economist,* January 4, 1997, pp. 57–58.

9. Howard Rothman, "Under pressure," *Business Ethics*, September/October 1996, pp.14–17.

10. "Why so many mergers miss the mark," *The Economist*, January 4, 1997, pp. 57–58.

11. Ibid.

12. Robert P. Bauman, Peter Jackson, and Joanne T. Lawrence, *From Promise to Performance: A Journey of Transformation at SmithKline Beecham* (Boston, MA: Harvard Business School Press, 1997), p. 3.

13. Ibid.

14. Robert Levering and Milton Moskowitz, *The 100 Best Companies to Work for in America* (New York: Currency Doubleday, 1993), p. 121.

15. Robert P. Bauman, Peter Jackson, and Joanne T. Lawrence, *From Promise to Performance: A Journey of Transformation at SmithKline Beecham* (Boston, MA: Harvard Business School Press, 1997).

16. Jack Canfield, Mark Victor Hansen, Maida Rogerson, Martin Rutte, and Tim Claus, *Chicken Soup for the Soul at Work* (Deerfield Beach, FL: Health Communications Inc., 1996), pp. 46–47.

17. Robert Levering and Milton Moskowitz, *The 100 Best Companies to Work for in America* (New York: Currency Doubleday, 1993), p. 122.

6

Vision, Mission, and Values

Vision deals with those deeper human intangibles that alone give ultimate purpose to life. In the end vision must always deal with life's qualities, not its quantities.

—William van Dusen Wishard

I think many people assume, wrongly, that a company exists simply to make money. While this is an important result of a company's existence, we have to go deeper and find the real reasons for our being.

—David Packard, Hewlett-Packard

As long as we keep purpose in focus in both our organizational and private lives, we are able to wander through the realms of chaos, make decisions about what actions will be consistent with our purpose, and emerge with a discernible pattern or shape to our lives.

—Margaret Wheatley

For most organizations, building a values-driven culture requires a shift in organizational consciousness from a world view that focuses on self-interest to a world view that focuses on the common good. This shift involves both personal and organizational transformation.

Three important changes take place during organizational transformation: (a) the organization moves from being profit-driven to being values-driven; (b) it begins to measure success in terms of its physical, emotional, mental, and spiritual health; and (c) the role of managers changes from being predominantly controlling to being predominantly empowering. Each of these aspects of transformation will be examined in the next three chapters. This chapter focuses on developing a values-driven organization.

VALUES-DRIVEN ORGANIZATIONS

When an organization moves from being profit-driven to being values-driven, it does not mean that it suddenly regards profit as unimportant. On the contrary. Profit remains a fundamental objective. In values-driven organizations the profit motive is contained within an overarching ethical framework. Limits are drawn as to what the organization will and will not do to make an extra dollar. Organizations that operate primarily from the lower levels of corporate consciousness often allow profit to take precedence over moral considerations. Organizations operating from higher levels of consciousness do not. In such organizations moral and ethical considerations take precedence. When an organization moves to this higher ground, the organization's values becomes pervasive—they affect everything it does. The values are carefully chosen to support the organization's vision and mission. Creating authentic and inspiring vision and mission statements is the first step in building a values-driven organization.

In reality, all organizations are values-driven. The critical issue is whether these values are conscious, shared and lived, or remain unconscious and undiscussed. When values are not defined, the culture of the organization is subject to the vagaries of the personality of the leader. When the leader changes, the values will change accordingly, particularly if the new leader is from outside the organization. If the personality of the leader is focused in the lower levels of consciousness, then the organization will operate from self-interest. If the personality of the leader is focused in the higher levels of consciousness, then the organization will operate for the common good.

Visionary organizations are not only aware of their values, they consciously use them to guide decision-making and to build a cohesive corporate culture. Visionary organizations find a dynamic balance between the organization's needs for survival and growth, the employees' needs for personal fulfillment, and the local community's and society's needs for economic, social, and environmental sustainability.

A strong positive culture is one of the six attributes of companies that have long-lasting financial success. Surprisingly few companies have such cultures. This could be due to several reasons:

- The company has not defined its vision, mission, and values.
- The management team has developed vision, mission, and values statements that have not been shared with employees.
- The company's vision, mission, and values have been defined, shared with employees, but not owned by them. Employees have not been given the opportunity to comment or participate in the process.
- The company's vision, mission, and values have been defined, are owned by the employees, but have not been integrated into the organization's systems, procedures, or practices. A strong positive culture can be established only if the values and concomitant behaviors are structurally integrated into the human resource systems, particularly the personnel evaluation processes. A values-based performance evaluation process and hiring policy are essential for developing a strong, positive culture.

Another reason why companies fail to develop strong positive cultures is that their vision, mission, and values statements are either too wordy or uninspiring. They lack motivational content. Three important questions must be addressed when building vision, mission, and values statements. What is the purpose of the statement? Who is the audience? and What should the statement do for that audience?

Vision

What Is the Purpose of a Vision Statement?

The primary purpose of a vision statement is to *describe how an organization finds its fulfillment*. It declares the company's intention with regard to the future it desires to create. The vision represents a deeper level of motivation than a mission. The mission describes the "means," the vision describes the "end." It makes a compelling statement about what the company is striving to achieve. Trammell Crow's vision for its future is very clear:

> "To be the premier customer-driven real estate services company in the U.S."

Whom Should the Vision Statement Address?

The vision should primarily address the needs of employees and society. They both want to know if the future the company wants to create resonates with their motivations and concerns. The vision is particularly important for employees, because it describes where the company might take them. No one wants to waste their time working toward a vision that does not motivate or inspire them. Society also wants to know that a company's products and services are environmentally friendly, that the company cares about social issues, and that it is making a positive difference in the world.

What Should the Vision Statement Do for Its Audience?

The tasks of a vision statement are to create a long-term motivational alignment between employees and the organization and generate societal goodwill. Alignment comes from a sense of shared vision. This leads to resonance, which generates goodwill. Resonance occurs at the level of shared beliefs about what is important. Goodwill occurs at the level of behaviors. Visions are particularly powerful in a motivational sense when they are shared by a group of people. Increasingly, companies that develop strong brand names do so on the strength of their societal vision and the role they play in making the world a better place to live.

Mission

What Is the Purpose of a Mission Statement?

Mission statements do two things. They keep the energies of the company focused around its core business, and they motivate stakeholders.

Once a company is successful, it often faces the temptation to expand into new sectors of activity. When this happens the energies can become diffuse and the company can lose its competitive edge in its core competence. Therefore, one of *the primary purposes of a mission statement is to declare the company's core business*. Steelcase, a provider of office furniture, provides a good example of a mission statement that declares its core business.

Helping people work more effectively.

The mission statement is concise, inclusive, and easily memorized. It achieves four objectives. It clearly states the company's core business, it allows room for expansion into efficiency-inducing products and services, it inspires customers, and at the same time it encourages Steelcase's own staff to work more effectively.

Avis also has a concise mission statement:

Our business is renting cars; our mission is total customer satisfaction.

It identifies the core business, and it leaves customers in no doubt that Avis cares about their needs. It sends a strong message to its employees that caring for customers is the company's number one concern.

The only exception to the rule that a mission statement should declare the organization's core business would be for a holding company or conglomerate. Its mission statement should reflect values that apply to all companies in the group. General Electric, for example, has a mission statement that comprises three values—boundaryless, speed, and stretch. In addition to the overarching values, each company in a conglomerate should have a vision and mission statement that identifies its core business and inspires employees, customers, and society.

Whom Should the Mission Statement Address?

In the past, most mission statements were directed toward three stakeholders—employees, customers, and stockholders. More and more mission statements are now also directed to society at large.

Intel uses the traditional three-prong approach, "Do a great job for our customers, employees, and stockholders by being the preeminent building block supplier to the computing industry."

Merck, on the other hand, prefers the four-prong model, putting society first, customers second, employees third, and stockholders last. The mission of Merck & Co. is:

> To provide society with superior products and services—innovations and solutions that satisfy customers needs and improve the quality of life—to provide employees with meaningful work and advancement opportunities and investors with a superior rate of return.

The issue of whom the mission statement addresses is important because it sets the tone for the organization's relationship with that group. Because of the growing importance of human capital and societal goodwill to a company's success, mission statements should address in priority order employees, customers, society, and stockholders. Stockholders are placed last because intelligent stockholders know that return on investment and shareholder value will be met if the company successfully meets the needs of the other groups first.

What Should the Mission Statement Do for Its Audience?

The mission statement should inspire employees and resonate with their inner motivations. It should also align with customers' concerns. Employees want to find personal fulfillment through their work. Customers want superior products and services that are affordable, environmentally friendly, and produced under conditions that do not degrade human dignity. Thus, the second purpose of the mission statement is to declare a company's intention with regard to meeting the needs of its stakeholders.

When companies are specific about how they will treat their stakeholders, they create a two-way pact of trust. Of course, they have to live up to those values or the trust will be broken. Becoming a values-driven organization is not easy. It demands the highest levels of integrity from its leaders, managers, and supervisors.

Values

What Is the Purpose of Values?

This is like asking what is the purpose of the Ten Commandments. *Values are rules for living.* They are deeply held beliefs that a certain way of being or a certain outcome is preferable to another. Values are externally demonstrated through behaviors. The phrase "walking the talk" means that there is no discrepancy between an individual's values and behaviors. Values "talk." Behaviors "walk." An organization's values make an open declaration about how it expects everyone in the organization to behave—no exceptions for leaders or managers.

In organizations with positive strong corporate cultures, the values become the rules of membership of the organization. If you live up to the values and get results, then you move onward and upward. If you live up to the values but don't get results, then you will be asked to take skills training. If you are unable to live up to the values but get results, you will be asked to take behavior training. If you are unable to live up to the values and don't get results, then you will be out.

The purpose of establishing a set of values is *to create a code of behavior that builds a cohesive culture and supports the vision and mission.* The values provide a framework within which every member of the organization can operate with responsible freedom. When individuals fully embrace the organization's values, everyone becomes mutually accountable.

Whom Should the Values Statement Address?

The primary audience for the values statement is the employees. Values are similar to the rules that enable birds to flock and fish to swim in shoals. When birds get together in large groups they fly as if they were one. The flock acts as a single cohesive entity, descending and ascending, swooping and landing as if they were all operating under the same instructions. It has been discovered through the use of computer simulation models that the rules of flocking are rules of behavior that apply to each individual bird.

The rules are simple. Each bird attempts to keep a minimum distance from its neighbors, to travel at the same velocity as its neighbors, to move toward the center of gravity of the birds in its vicinity, and to keep away from fixed objects. These rules of behavior are the "values" that birds live by when they behave as a cohesive entity. When every individual employee lives by the organization's values, they become a cohesive unit, just like a flock of birds. Trust is created because everyone is living by the same credo.

What Do Values Do?

Values that are shared build trust and create community. They also create cohesion and unity. Strong communities are characterized by sincere friendliness and the ability to pursue shared objectives quickly and efficiently. *The strength of a community depends on the commitment of its individual members to live by the shared rules.* When values are not shared, there is no sense of community. Taken to the extreme, lack of shared values creates anarchy. To create a strong corporate culture, the values must be lived by everyone, most importantly by those in leadership or power positions. A strong core culture can be created only when there is alignment between values and behaviors at all levels of the organization.

Motivational Content of Statement

Vision, mission, and values statements relate to specific levels of corporate consciousness and a specific audience. The ability to categorize statements in this way provides a useful tool for checking whether the organization's statements are well balanced and address the needs of all stakeholders. Table 6–1 gives examples of vision and mission statements and shows how they relate to specific levels of consciousness and specific audiences.

Table 6-1

Relationship of Mission Statements to the Seven Levels of Corporate Consciousness

MOTIVATION/LEVEL AUDIENCE	COMPANY	STATEMENT
Service—Level 7 Audience: Society	Merck	We are in the business of preserving and improving human life.
	Ben & Jerry's	To operate the company in a way that actively recognizes the central role that business plays in the structure of society by initiating innovative ways to improve the quality of life of a broad community—local, national, and international.
	Hewlett-Packard	Our main task is to design, develop, and manufacture the finest electronic equipment for the advancement of science and the welfare of humanity.
Making a Difference— Level 6 Audience: Customers and Community	Steelcase	Helping people work more effectively.
	Hanna Andersson	To enhance the richly textured experience of family and community.
Meaning—Level 5 Audience: Employees	Sony	Respect and encourage each individual's ability and creativity.
	Tom's of Maine	To provide meaningful work, fair compensation, and a safe healthy work environment that encourages openness, creativity, self-discipline, and growth.
Transformation—Level 4 Audience: Employees	3M	Respect for individual initiative and personal growth.
	Motorola	Continuous self-renewal.
Self-Esteem—Level 3 Audience: Employees	Georgia Pacific	Being the best at everything we do.
	Trammel Crow Company	To be the premier customer-driven real estate services company in the U.S.
	General Mills	The company of champions.
Survival/Growth— Level 1 Audience: Stockholders	Kellogg	Profitable growth is our primary purpose.

	Personal Motivation	Organization: Internal Motivation	Organization: External Motivation
Vision	Self Fulfillment	Organization Fulfillment	Societal Contribution
Mission	Self Development	Organization Development	Service to Customers
Values	Personal Values	Internal Values	External Values

Figure 6–1
Overview of the Four Why's Process

THE "FOUR WHY'S"

Now that we have defined the purpose, audience, and desired impact of vision, mission, and values statements and shown how they relate to the seven levels of corporate consciousness, I want to describe a method for creating statements that address the specific needs of employees, customers, and society. The method is called the "Four Why's."

The process differs from other methods in that it (a) differentiates between an organization's internal motivations and its external motivations, (b) addresses the needs of employees, customers, and society, and (c) builds a motivational link between employees' personal motivations and the organization's motivations. Figure 6–1 presents an overview of the process.

I propose to describe the process by referring to the establishment of the vision, mission, and values for Richard Barrett & Associates LLC.

Internal Motivation

The Internal Mission

Step 1: Two important questions must be answered to discover the internal mission of an organization: (a) *"What is our core business?"* and (b) *"What do we need to do to grow and develop as an organization?"* The answer to the first question gives focus to our work. The answer to the second question provides us with an inspirational statement that motivates employees. After some discussion, we decided that Richard Barrett & Associates LLC was in the business of *values-driven organizational transformation* and that the company will grow and develop by *building a worldwide community of professionals committed to values-driven organizational transformation*. Therefore our internal mission is: *To build a worldwide community of professionals committed to values-driven organizational transformation.*

The Internal Vision

Step 2: The next step is to develop a statement that describes organizational fulfillment. We arrive at this statement by asking *"Why?"* in front of our internal mission. The answer represents a deeper level of motivation. We asked the question *"Why do we want to build a worldwide community of professionals committed to values-driven organizational transformation?"* The answer: *"To be a global resource for organizational transformation."* This is our internal vision and the answer to the first "Why." These two statements together—the internal mission and the internal vision—provide a direction for the development and growth of the organization and its employees. Figure 6–2 illustrates the process used in defining the internal motivations.

If we were to go to the internal vision and ask *"How are we going to become a global resource for organizational transformation?"* we would find the answer in our internal mission—*"by building a worldwide community of professionals committed to values-driven organizational transformation."* This is an important concept. To get to a deeper level of motivation ask, *"Why?"* To move back ask, *"How?"*

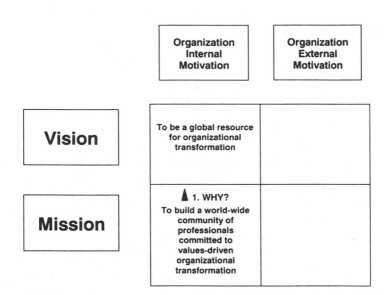

Figure 6–2
Defining the Internal Mission and Vision

If, for example, an organization already has a good internal vision but does not have an internal mission, then ask the question *"How?"* in front of the internal vision. This will lead you to the internal mission.

External Motivation

The External Mission
Step 3: After defining the internal mission and vision, the next step is to discover the external mission. This is an inspirational statement that describes the service we provide to our clients. Again we asked the question *"Why?"* in front of the internal mission. *"Why* do we want *to build a worldwide community of professionals committed to values-driven organizational transformation?"* The desired answer is a statement that will inspire our customers. Our answer was *"To support leaders in building visionary organizations."* This is our external mission and the answer to the second "Why."

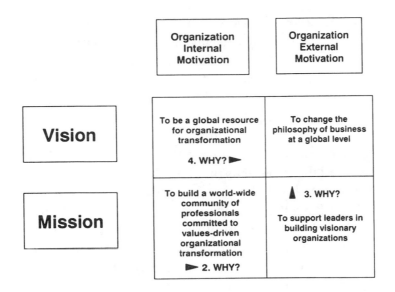

Figure 6–3
Defining the External Mission and Vision

The External Vision
Step 4: The next step is to discover the external vision. This is an inspirational statement that describes the contribution we want to make to society. To get to this statement we need to ask the question *"Why?"* in front of our external mission. *"Why do we want to support leaders in building visionary organizations?"* The answer is, *"To change the philosophy of business at a global level."* This is our external vision and the answer to the third "Why." These two statements together—the external mission and the external vision—explain how we are going to assist our customers and the benefits that this will bring to society. Figure 6–3 illustrates the process used in defining the external motivations.

If an organization has an external vision but no external mission, the question *"How?"* can be used in front of the external vision to find its external mission.

We can now do a check on the internal consistency of the external vision by asking the question *"Why?"* in front of the internal vision. The external vision should represent a deeper level of motivation of the internal vision. When we asked *"Why* do we want *to become a global resource for organizational transformation?"* We found that answer in the external mission—*"To change the philosophy of business at a global level."* This was the fourth "Why?" In this manner we have created a continuous motivational loop that links all four statements together.

The team working on the mission and vision will know when they have reached closure because there will be a strong resonance around the statements that have been developed. If the resonance is absent, the work is not finished.

In Richard Barrett & Associates LLC we believe that by building a worldwide community of professionals committed to values-driven organizational transformation, we can become a global resource for corporate transformation. We want to become a global resource so that we can help leaders all over the world build visionary organizations. This supports our external vision of changing the philosophy of business at a global level.

Values

Values That Support Internal Motivations

Step 5: The next step is to define the values that will support the internal motivations. This is done by reaching consensus on the values we believe will support us in achieving our internal mission and vision. The values we chose to support us in achieving our internal mission—*to build a worldwide community of professionals committed to values-driven organizational transformation*—were excellence, innovation, and profit. The values chosen to support us in achieving our internal vision—*to be a global resource for organizational transformation*—were trust and strategic alliances.

Excellence responds to the need to be professional. Innovation responds to need to continue to grow and develop our corporate transformation models and tools. Profit responds to our need to find right livelihood through our work, invest in the continuing development of the corporate transformation models and tools, build a global transformation network, and create a sufficient surplus to be able to carry out pro bono work for not-for-profit organizations. Trust is important in creating organizational cohesion, and strategic alliances are important in building a worldwide network of partnerships with consultants and human resource specialists who will be working with the corporate transformation models and tools.

Values That Support External Motivations

Step 6: The next step is to define the values that will support the external motivations. This is done by reaching consensus on the values we believe will support us in achieving our external mission and vision. The values we chose to support us in achieving our external mission—*to support leaders in building visionary organizations*—were service and empowerment. The values we chose to support us in achieving our external vision—*to change the philosophy of business at a global level*—were ethics and the evolution of consciousness.

We want to be of service to leaders by empowering them and their organizations to become all they can become. In this way we hope to contribute to the evolution of consciousness. Ethics responds to our need always to be driven by the highest possible motivations in our work.

More Why's

Departmental Motivations and Values

Step 7: Steps 1 through 6 are usually carried out by the management team. The next step is to elicit feedback from the rest of the organization. This is done by sharing the statements with the next level of management (departmental heads) and asking them to build their departmental mission statements. When they ask "Why?" in front of their departmental mission statements they should find the answer in the organizational level statements. If they don't, then they may want to modify their own statements or suggest modifications to the organizational level statements. The departments should also reflect on their values. They should either endorse the organization's chosen values or suggest alternatives.

Personal Motivation

Step 8: The final step is to build a motivational connection between the mission of every individual and the mission of the organization. When an individual asks "Why?" in front of his or her personal mission statement, the individual should find the answer in the department's or organization's statement. It is important to realize that it is not necessary to link one's personal mission to the mission of the unit where one works. A personal motivation could relate to the departmental or organizational mission.

If when you ask "Why? in front of your personal mission you don't find the answer in the department's or organization's mission or vision, then the motivational link is broken. In this case, you will not find fulfillment in the organization. There must always be a motivational link between a personal mission and some level of the organization's vision and mission for fulfillment to be found. It is in the organization's best interest to help every individual find work that makes this link. When an individual's motivation and an organization's motivation are aligned, then people tap into their deepest levels of productivity and creativity. Mission mentality then becomes a competitive advantage.

By the time this exercise is completed, every individual and department should have a clear mission statement and know how they relate to the organization's mission and vision in a logical motivational chain. At this point, the management team should do a consolidation check to make sure the department's and the organization's statements are in alignment. When this has been done, and any necessary adjustments made, a communications strategy can be developed to tell the staff about the organization's vision, mission, and values.

The Importance of Aligning Personal and Organizational Missions and Visions

While employee participation in the creation of the organizational mission and vision is important, it is even more important that individuals are able to make a direct link between their personal motivations and the organization's motivations. Individuals will move into alignment with an organization's vision or mission only if they are able to pursue their own mission within the framework of the organization's vision and mission.

I would submit therefore that it is not the sharing of an organizational mission or vision that creates cohesion, but *the creation of opportunities within the organizational mission for every individual to find work that corresponds to his or her personal mission or vision.* This is what creates alignment. Employees want work that brings meaning to their lives, and they also want to see how their contributions make a difference to the well-being of the organization as a whole and society at large.

The Best Starting Point for the "Four Why's" Process

The best way for a management team to prepare for the Four Why's exercise is first to develop their personal mission and vision statements. These statements should then be shared. Simply listening to the missions and visions of colleagues will begin to create a sense of cohesion and trust. Points of convergence and divergence should be noted and discussed. This information will assist the team in reaching consensus on the organization's vision, mission, and values.

Core Motivations

One of the best ways to develop the personal missions of the management team is to follow the Core Motivation method. This is most effective when it is done as a group exercise. Each member of the management team writes down at the top of a piece of paper the following statement: *I come to work each day because I want to* _____ . They fill in the blank with a statement about what motivates them about their work. Let us call this statement *AAA*. At this point every member of the management team reads aloud the statement they have written.

Everyone then finds a partner and gives their piece of paper with the *AAA* statement on it to that person. Each partner then probes to find out why the other wants to *AAA* and writes down the response as *BBB* immediately below the statement *AAA*. When both partners have written down their partner's *BBB* statements, then the partners probe again to find out why they want to *BBB*. The answer is recorded as *CCC*. When both partners have completed their *CCC* statements, the process is repeated and their *DDD* statements are recorded.

At this point the papers are returned to their originators and each person reads aloud their *DDD* statement. This is best done continuously without comment until everyone has finished. There will be a very noticeable difference between the *AAA* statements and the *DDD* statements. You will find that the *DDD* statements tend to converge to one or two simple themes. These themes can either be used as the starting point for the Four Why's process or can be integrated as one of the four motivational statements. The convergence is due to the fact that every time you ask why, you move to a deeper level of motivation. At these deeper levels of motivation we always find themes that are common to humanity. People often remark after this exercise that they feel that they have shared their souls.

Advantages of the "Four Why's" Process

The "Four Why's" process of building vision, mission, and values statements offers several advantages:

1. The separation of the internal and external motivations gives greater clarity to the mission and vision statements by separating the needs of employees from the needs of customers and society.

2. The linking of statements in a motivational chain creates internal consistency.

3. The process allows everyone in the organization to relate their personal mission to the organization's mission or vision. All employees can see exactly how they and their department make a difference in serving the greater whole.

4. Linking the "Four Why's" process to the Seven Levels of Corporate Consciousness makes it possible to engineer vision, mission, and values statements that address the needs of all stakeholders and develop a healthy distribution of organizational consciousness.

Mission Before Vision

There are two reasons why an organization's mission statement should precede the vision statement. First, it is important to make sure that everyone in the organization is in complete agreement about the organization's core business. I have worked in several large organizations in which vice presidents marched to different tunes. The result was a lack of focus and a diluting of energies. The vice presidents were able to pursue their personal interests because the mandate of the organization was too diffuse.

Second, it is important for individuals and organizations to get in touch with their deepest purpose (mission) before they get in touch with their vision. A vision without a mission often results in the dispersion of energies and ineffectual performance. Understanding your mission requires a profound knowledge of self.

Presenting the Values

An important consideration in drafting the final version of the values is the presentational format. Some organizations simply state their values in the form of a mission statement. Harley Davidson, for example, lists its values:

Be fair.

Tell the truth.

Keep your promises.

Respect the individual.

Encourage intellectual curiosity.

Another popular way to present values is to put them in the form of general statements of intention. Here are examples from Merck and Intel. I have italicized what I believe are their essential values.

MERCK. We are committed to the highest standards of *ethics* and *integrity*. We are *responsible* to our customers, to our employees, to the environments we inhabit, and to the societies we serve around the world. In discharging our responsibilities, we *do not take professional or ethical shortcuts*. Our interactions with our environments and with all segments of society—our customers, our suppliers, governments, and general public—must reflect the *highest standards* we profess.

INTEL. Customer Orientation: *Partnerships* with our customers and suppliers are essential to our mutual success. We strive to:

- *Listen* to our customers.
- *Communicate mutual intentions* and expectations.
- Deliver *innovative* and *competitive* products and services.
- Make it *easy* to work with us.
- Serve our customers through *partnerships with our suppliers*.

A third way to present values is in the form of a credo. Here is an example from Tom's of Maine.

WE BELIEVE that both human beings and nature have inherent worth and deserve our *respect*.

WE BELIEVE in products that are *safe*, *effective*, and made of *natural* ingredients.

WE BELIEVE that our company and our products are unique and worthwhile and that we can sustain these genuine qualities with an ongoing commitment to *innovation* and *creativity*.

WE BELIEVE that we have a *responsibility* to cultivate the *best relationships* possible with our co-workers, customers, owners, agents, suppliers, and our community.

WE BELIEVE in providing employees with a *safe* and *fulfilling* work environment, and an opportunity to *grow* and *learn*.

WE BELIEVE that our company can be *financially successful* while behaving in a *socially responsible* and *environmentally sensitive* manner.

In the end, the manner in which the values are presented is a matter of personal preference. The first method is easy to remember and can be easily fitted onto a card that can be kept in a wallet or purse. The second method provides context for the values, but the statements are not easy to remember. The third method is similar to the second.

The "Four Why's" process provides a powerful systematic framework for defining the organization's core business and how it will find internal and external fulfillment. It facilitates the process of developing inspirational vision, mission, and values statements that link the motivations of the organization to the motivations of its stakeholders. The method brings clarity to the process and is simple to use. In the next chapter we will discuss how the "Four Why's" process is used in dynamic interaction with a Balanced Needs Scorecard to develop strategic goals that support the organization's physical, emotional, mental, and spiritual health.

7

Balance

Most companies are still dominated by numbers, information and analysis. That makes it much harder to tap into intuition, feelings, and nonlinear thinking—the skills that leaders will need to succeed in the future.

—MORT MEYERSON, CHAIRMAN, PEROT SYSTEMS

If you want to change your company, change how it relates to customers. When we launch a new product, we identify a collection of early adopters and christen them "pioneers." We talk to them. We find out what's working and not working. As we discover bugs and fix them in subsequent revisions, we go back to our pioneers and upgrade their machines for free. The effect is a sustained dialogue that benefits both sides.

—JIM TAYLOR, SR. VICE PRESIDENT, GATEWAY 2000

The Balanced Scorecard helps organizations move from being financially driven to being mission driven.

—DAVID P. NORTON, PRESIDENT OF RENAISSANCE SOLUTIONS

In the *Seven Habits of Highly Effective People*, Stephen Covey writes, "True effectiveness requires balance."[1] According to Covey, we become really effective only when we take care of our physical, mental, emotional, and spiritual needs. He writes, "Although renewal in each dimension is important, it only becomes optimally effective as we deal with all four dimensions in a wise and balanced way. To neglect any one area negatively impacts on the rest. I have found this to be true in organizations as well as in individual lives. In an organization the physical is expressed in economic

125

terms. The mental or psychological dimension deals with recognition, development, and use of talent. The social/emotional dimension has to do with human relationships, with how people are treated. And the spiritual dimension deals with finding meaning through purpose or contribution and through organizational integrity." [2] What Covey is suggesting is that organizations are more effective when they take a holistic approach to balancing their needs.

Although Covey's personal balancing system is being used by millions to improve their effectiveness at work, there is no widespread holistic balancing system to improve organizational effectiveness. The closest we have to such a system is the Balanced Scorecard developed by Robert Kaplan of the Harvard Business School and David Norton of the Renaissance Strategy Group.[3] The Balanced Scorecard focuses on four aspects of performance: the financial perspective, the customer perspective, the internal business—process perspective, and the learning and growth perspective. It does not directly address the cultural perspective, the supplier perspective, and the organization's role in the local community and society. To be truly effective the Balanced Scorecard should address all these perspectives. It should also be values driven. This chapter is devoted to developing a six-part Balanced Needs Scorecard that expands and builds on the concept of the Balanced Scorecard.

THE BALANCED NEEDS SCORECARD

The first three categories of the Balanced Need Scorecard represent the primary needs of an organization: Corporate Survival—profits, finance, and funding; Corporate Fitness—productivity, quality, and efficiency; and Customer/Supplier Relations—sales, service, and product excellence. These are fundamental issues for the successful operation of every business and organization. They represent the "hard stuff." The next three categories support these front-line needs. They include Corporate Evolution—participation, innovation, and

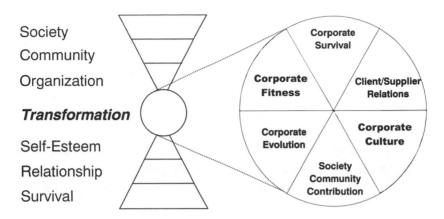

Figure 7-1
The Six Categories of the Balanced Needs Scorecard

creativity; Corporate Culture—vision, mission, values, and employee fulfillment; and Society and Community Contribution—social and environmental responsibility, being of service, and making a difference. They represent the "soft stuff." In the twenty-first century the soft stuff is destined to become the hard stuff. Enlightened organizations know that corporate culture, society, and community contributions are the next arenas of competitive advantage. The six categories of the Balanced Needs Scorecard are shown in Figure 7–1 and key indicators in each category are described next.

Corporate Survival

Performance in this category is measured in terms of financial or growth indicators. The indicators may vary during the life cycle of the organization. A start-up company, for example, may set goals related to capital formation. A well-established company may focus on goals related to profit, return on assets, and cash reserves. A public company may want to measure its success by its stock price. Growth indicators in the service sector may relate to number of customers or number of outlets. This category corresponds to an organization's physical needs.

Corporate Fitness

Performance in this category is measured by indicators that relate to improving systems and processes—speed, cycle time, quality, productivity, and efficiency. The most important of these processes are those that affect customers, finances, and employee productivity. Thus, the time between order taking and delivery, the time between order taking and payment, and the output per employee are popular targets for improving corporate fitness. The targets are usually achieved through some form of reengineering. This category corresponds partially to an organization's emotional needs.

Customer/Supplier Relations

Performance in this category is measured by indicators related to market share, brand loyalty, customer satisfaction, and customer collaboration. Indicators that relate to supplier relations are also important. The values audit instrument can be used to measure the quality of customer and supplier relations. It can also be used to measure the degree of values alignment between the organization and its customers and suppliers. This category corresponds partially to an organization's emotional and spiritual needs.

Corporate Evolution

Performance in this category is measured by indicators that relate to how well the organization is doing in generating ideas that result in product and process innovation—creating new products and services, adapting existing products and services, and generating ideas that improve internal processes. The indicators chosen should reflect the organization's goals for improving employee participation, research and development, developing an innovation pipeline, and learning and knowledge. This category corresponds to an organization's mental needs.

Corporate Culture

Performance in this category is measured by indicators that relate to vision, mission, values, and employee fulfillment. The values audit instrument allows organizations to measure the degree of alignment between personal and organizational values, organizational and ideal organizational values, and actual and espoused values, as well as the strength and type of core culture. Key indicators might include the CTS index, the PTOS index, the PN index, and the ST index. This category corresponds partially to an organization's emotional and spiritual needs.

Society/Community Contribution

Performance in this category is measured by indicators that relate to social and environmental responsibility. Key indicators in this category might include the number of volunteer hours worked by employees for the local community and measures of the impact that the organization is having through its outreach programs to the local community and society at large. This category corresponds partially to an organization's spiritual needs.

The Internal Logic of the Balanced Needs Scorecard

Viewed from a systems perspective, the six categories of the Balanced Needs Scorecard form an interactive chain of cause and effect. The chain of linkages is shown diagrammatically in Figure 7–2.

Corporate Survival

Profitability and growth depend directly on sales (Customer Relationships) and productivity (Corporate Fitness). These in turn are dependent on employee fulfillment (Corporate Culture), product innovation (Corporate Evolution), and societal goodwill (Society and Community Contribution). When organizations achieve profitability they are not only able to pay dividends to their shareholders, they can also increase their investment in employee fulfillment (Corporate Culture), process and product innovation (Corporate Evolution), customer and supplier relationships, and contributions to the local community and society at large. As they reinvest in these five areas, they increase their chances of becoming even more profitable.

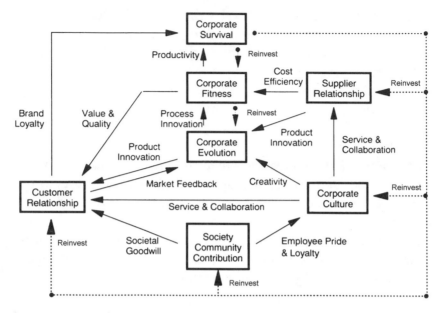

Figure 7–2
A Systems Perspective of the Balanced Needs Scorecard

Corporate Fitness

When organizations focus on internal processes and systems, they increase productivity, efficiency, and quality. Improvements in productivity improve profitability. Improvements in efficiency affect price. Improvements in price and quality improve value to customers.

Customer and Supplier Relationships

When organizations enter into collaborative relationships with customers, they learn how to increase customer satisfaction by innovating and designing their products and services to better meet their customers' needs. When organizations enter into collaborative relationships with suppliers, they not only find ways of cutting costs and improving quality of products but also increase the possibility of increasing product innovation. The quality and price advantages translate into increased value to customers.

Corporate Evolution

When organizations are open to feedback from customer collaboration, have cultures that support employee creativity, and invest in research and development, they are able to innovate continually. Organizations that focus on evolution create a stream of innovation that becomes the future lifeblood of the organization. This innovation can take the form of new and improved products and services or of improved processes.

Corporate Culture

When organizations focus on building a strong corporate identity and a culture that supports employee fulfillment, they improve customer satisfaction and supplier collaboration. Improvements in employee fulfillment also increase creativity and motivation, thus enhancing corporate evolution.

Society and Community Contribution

When organizations support their local communities and become involved in improving conditions for disadvantaged members of society or the environment, they build societal and customer goodwill and employee pride. Employee pride helps to build employee loyalty. Employee motivation is also enhanced by creating opportunities for work in the local community. Both of these have a positive impact on the corporate culture. Organizations often choose to support issues that are linked to the concerns of their customers. For example, outdoor equipment manufacturers support environmental causes. Customers who are concerned about specific issues will tend to support companies that care about the same issues.

Brand Loyalty

One of the major goals of the Balanced Needs Scorecard is to build strategies that increase brand loyalty. All six categories of the scorecard can be used:

- Improving corporate culture improves employee fulfillment, which in turn improves customer relations.

- Improving supplier collaboration improves corporate fitness, which in turn increases quality and value to customers.
- Improving corporate evolution increases product innovation.
- Improving the organization's contribution to the local community and society improves customer goodwill.
- Improving profits increases the amount of money available to improve every other category of the scorecard.

We are rapidly approaching a time when it will be impossible to build a successful brand without creating a socially and environmentally responsible organization. Who you are and what your organization stands for are becoming just as important as the quality and technological sophistication of what you sell. As more and more companies enter the global marketplace, it is becoming increasingly difficult to compete on technological advantage alone. Competitive advantage will gradually shift from purely technological superiority to a mixture of technological *and* values superiority. Increasingly, customers are preferring to buy products made by socially and environmentally aware companies when quality and price are equal. This will mean that in the future brand building will become integrally linked with culture building. The two will become inseparable. The awareness of society is such that companies will no longer be able to hide behind the facade of values that advertising agencies create to sell their products. Society is demanding and looking for corporate integrity.

Lead and Lag Indicators

In addition to the valuable contribution that Kaplan and Norton made in developing the Balanced Scorecard, they brought to the fore the importance of establishing indicators that contribute to improving future performance. Most standard indicators of financial performance measure results of actions that took place in the past. These are called lag indicators. They have no predictive powers for future performance. Lead indicators, on the other hand, measure progress on implementing improvements that can have a positive impact on future performance.

For example, a lead indicator for the category "corporate culture" could be the number of managers who have successfully completed an emotional intelligence training program. A lag indicator would measure the level of trust in the organization. Trust should increase if the managers implement their newly acquired emotional intelligence skills. There will be a delay between the training (lead indicator) and the impact of the training (lag indicator). In the same manner, customer collaboration is a lead indicator and customer satisfaction is a lag indicator. Ideally, a mixture of lead and lag indicators should be established for each category of the scorecard. Lead indicators usually measure inputs. Lag indicators usually measure outcomes or outputs (the impact of the inputs). When outcomes do not match the expectations of the inputs, take a hard look at the delivery and quality of inputs.

Because of the internal logic of the cause and effect of the Balanced Needs Scorecard, every category of the scorecard serves as a lead or a lag indicator to other categories. For example, improvements in Corporate Evolution affect Corporate Fitness through process innovation. Thus, improving Corporate Evolution will eventually improve Corporate Fitness. Similarly, improving Corporate Culture creates greater employee fulfillment, which affects Customer Relationships. The most important categories (those with the most linkages in the cause-effect chain) are Customer Relationships, Corporate Evolution (innovation), Corporate Culture (employee fulfillment), and Corporate Fitness (productivity).

Building a Balanced Needs Scorecard

The process of building a Balanced Needs Scorecard involves three stages:

- Stage 1: Develop the organization's internal and external mission and vision statements using the "Four Why's" process and identify the values that support each of these statements.
- Stage 2: Define goals for each category of the scorecard that support the vision and mission statements. Develop corresponding objectives and stretch targets for each goal. Identify

for each objective a set of lead and lag indicators that can be updated on a monthly or quarterly basis.

- Stage 3: Identify the values that support the objectives in each category of the Balanced Needs Scorecard. Compare these values with the values obtained from the "Four Why's" process. Adjust the organization's values to ensure that the values needed to implement the strategic goals of the Balanced Needs Scorecard are included.

The Balanced Needs Scorecard as a Diagnostic Tool

The Balanced Needs Scorecard can be used in conjunction with the values audit instrument as diagnostic tool to assess the degree of balance in the top ten values of the organization's existing culture. Many of the values in the organizational values template are directly related to specific categories of the scorecard. For example, the value "learning" is associated with the category "Corporate Evolution," and "trust" is associated with "Corporate Culture." Thus, it is possible by association to see which categories of the Balanced Needs Scorecard are important to the organization.

Figures 7–3 and 7–4 show the results for Companies A and B (the Values Audits for these companies are described in Chapter 5). The results clearly show that neither Company A nor Company B is particularly well balanced. The managers in Company A are focused on Corporate Evolution with some emphasis on Corporate Survival and Corporate Fitness. The staff in Company B, on the other hand, is very strongly focused on Corporate Culture and to a lesser extent on Society and Community Contribution and Corporate Survival. Company A has two of the three fundamental categories covered, Survival and Fitness, whereas Company B has only one fundamental category covered, Survival. Neither company has a customer focus. The strong culture of Company B is largely responsible for its success. This success could be precarious if the company doesn't become more focused on its customer relationships, corporate fitness, and corporate evolution. Company A is suffering financially

Company A

Organizational Values

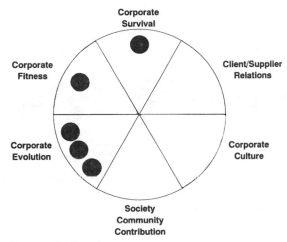

Figure 7–3
Company A: Balanced Needs Scorecard Diagnostic

Company B

Organizational Values

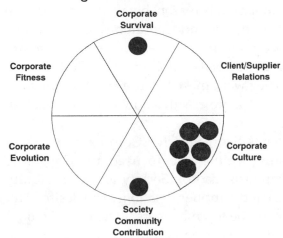

Figure 7–4
Company B: Balanced Needs Scorecard Diagnostic

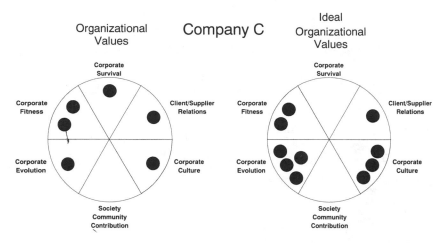

Figure 7–5
Company C: Balanced Needs Scorecard Diagnostic

because of its lack of focus on customer relationships and corporate culture. It also needs to do more in the area of Society and Community Contribution.

Figures 7–5 and 7–6 show a comparison of the Balanced Needs Scorecard diagnostics for the existing and desired organizational cultures of Companies C and D. The existing Balanced Needs Scorecard of Company C is reasonably well balanced. The only category missing is Society and Community Contribution. The Balanced Needs Scorecard for the ideal organization shows that the managers want to focus on Corporate Culture and Corporate Evolution. They want more balance and fulfillment in their lives. They also want more creativity, innovation, and risk taking.

The Balanced Needs Scorecard for Company D clearly shows that the existing values are focused on Corporate Culture with some emphasis also on Society and Community Contribution and Client and Supplier Relations. The desired culture as expressed through the top managers' ideal organizational values is heavily focused on Corporate Survival and Corporate Fitness with some emphasis on Corporate Evolution. None of these three categories are covered by the values of the current

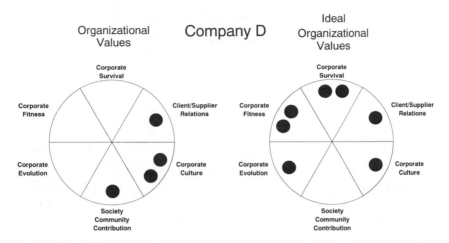

Figure 7–6
Company D: Balanced Needs Scorecard Diagnostic

culture. The difference between the existing and ideal organizational values clearly reflects the managers' desire to get more organized.

Measurement Motivates

An important attribute of the Balanced Needs Scorecard approach is its ability to link individual and work unit targets to the organization's goals. Once goals have been set at the organizational level, each individual work unit can determine the objectives it needs to meet the organization's goals. Individuals in the work unit can then assess the targets they need to attain the work unit's objectives. In this way every individual can measure his or her contribution to the work unit's objectives and their work unit's contribution to the overall goals of the organization. Being able to measure how an individual or work unit is making a difference to the performance of the organization provides a motivational link between individual efforts and the success of the organization. When individual and work unit performance is measured against a set of objectives and targets, every individual is challenged to seek ways of improving the way in which they work. For optimal performance, targets should not be imposed but should be set by the work units and individuals concerned.

Evolutionary Thinking

Strategic goals set at the organizational level should stretch the minds and abilities of the organization. Goals that call for an increase in performance by a few percentage points promote "change thinking." These improvements can often be achieved by reengineering—doing what we do now, but doing it differently. Goals that call for quantum increases in performance promote "transformational thinking." These improvements are achieved only by taking a systems approach—a shift in basic assumptions that creates a new way of being and doing—evolution. Not doing things differently, but doing different things. When individuals are asked to participate in transformational thinking, they tap into their intuition and creativity. This type of thinking can be maintained only in corporate cultures that are built around trust, employee involvement, and openness. When high levels of trust are maintained and the organization systematically encourages employee involvement, then "evolutionary thinking" can take place.

LONG-LASTING SUCCESSFUL COMPANIES

The importance of balance in business has been confirmed by the research findings of Collins and Porras.[4] Their studies show that contrary to business school doctrine, maximizing shareholder wealth and profit maximization are not the dominant driving forces in most long-lasting successful companies. Successful companies pursue a cluster of objectives of which making money is only one—and not necessarily the primary one. They state, "Throughout the history of most visionary companies we saw a core ideology that transcended purely economic considerations."[5]

Their visionary companies[6] include 18 very well known large organizations that have been operating for more than 50 years—the youngest company being founded in 1945 and the oldest in 1812. What is striking about these companies is their financial performance. "Suppose you had made equal investments in a general-market stock fund, a comparison company stock fund, and a visionary company stock fund on January 1, 1926. If you reinvested all dividends and made appropriate adjustments for when companies became available on the Stock Exchange, your $1 in the general market fund would have grown to $415 on December 31, 1990. Your $1 invested in the group of comparison companies would have grown to $995—more than twice the general market. But your $1 in the visionary companies stock fund would have grown to $6,356—over six times the comparison fund and over fifteen times the general market."[7]

The long-lasting successful companies in Collins and Porras's research included American Express, 3M, Boeing, Citicorp, Ford, General Electric, Hewlett-Packard, and IBM.[8] The comparison companies included Wells Fargo, Norton, McDonnell Douglas, Chase Manhattan, General Motors, Westinghouse, Texas Instruments, and Burroughs.[9] Half of the 18 long-lasting successful companies are included in the latest edition of *The 100 Best Companies to Work for in America*. None of the comparison companies are included.

If these long-lasting companies are doing so well by pursuing a cluster of objectives, the important question is, what objectives are they pursuing? To answer this question I analyzed the summaries of the core ideologies of Collins and Porras's 18 long-lasting successful companies. Each of the statements of every company's core ideology was assigned to one of the six Balanced Needs Scorecard categories. In some cases a single statement yielded more than one category. In such cases, I allocated the statement to several categories. Of the 18 companies, 15 had objectives that covered three or more categories. The most frequently appearing category was Corporate Culture. Corporate Survival (profits or shareholder value) ranked last. Twenty-six percent of all statements referred to values that are consistent with promoting corporate culture—employee fulfillment, honesty, integrity, respect, commitment, enthusiasm, etc. The second highest scoring category was Corporate Fitness, with 20 percent of the

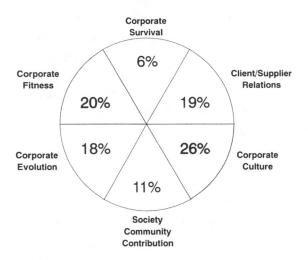

Based on Espoused
Organizational Values

Figure 7–7
Composite Balanced Needs Scorecard of 18 Long-Lasting Successful
Companies

statements. Customer/Supplier Relations ranked third with 19
percent of statements, and Corporate Evolution ranked fourth
with 18 percent. Only 6 out of the 18 companies had core ideologies that mentioned profits. The results of this analysis are shown
in Figure 7–7.

The conclusion I reach from this analysis is that financial success is directly related to the inputs an organization makes into
Corporate Fitness, Corporate Culture, Corporate Evolution,
Customer/Supplier Relations, and Society/Community Contributions. When organizations strive to increase profits by addressing
only one or two of these categories, long-term financial success
will not be sustainable. This is why reengineering has frequently
failed. It addressed only the organization's corporate fitness and
profitability needs. It did not address the organization's culture
needs. Similarly, learning organizations that focus on the organization's external mental needs will not meet with long-term suc-

cess if part of that learning is not directed inward to improving the organization's culture. The inner learning must be accompanied by changes in values and behaviors if the organization is to evolve and grow. A successful organization, like a successful individual, needs to be sensitive to all aspects of its well-being.

Many CEOs confirm that focusing on inputs works. Don Petersen, former CEO at Ford, put it this way: "Putting profits after people and products was magical at Ford."[10] John Young, former CEO of Hewlett-Packard, had a similar philosophy: "Profit is a cornerstone of what we do—it is a measure of our contribution and a means of self-financed growth—but it has never been the *point* in and of itself. . . . Profit is not *why* the Hewlett-Packard Company exists; it exists for more fundamental reasons."[11] Dave Packard, founder of Hewlett-Packard, was very clear about these reasons: "[We exist] first and foremost to make a contribution to society, and our main task is to design, develop, and manufacture the finest electronic [equipment] for the advancement of science and welfare of humanity."[12]

It stands to reason that the more actions that are taken to improve productivity, cost-effectiveness, quality, value to customers, collaboration with customers and suppliers, process and product innovation, creativity, goodwill, and contribution to society, the greater will be the profits. This is the purpose of the Balanced Needs Scorecard to systematically measure inputs and monitor the resulting outcomes.

This aligns with a profound spiritual principle—what you receive from the world is in direct measure to what you give to the world. When organizations care about employee fulfillment, customer satisfaction, and being responsible members of the community and good global citizens, they find that employees, customers, and society care about them. The result is increased profitability and stockholder returns. When an organization is strongly focused on getting rather than giving, it may be successful in the short-term, but it will not meet with long-term success. In the long run, miserly treatment of employees and pinch-penny service to customers will undermine attempts to be profitable.

As stated in the introduction to this chapter, balance—an important aspect of Level 4 consciousness—is a prerequisite for corporate transformation. It is impossible to shift successfully from a culture of self-interest to a culture that supports the common good without first attaining balance. In the following chapter we will discuss four of the most important values for creating cultures that support the common good—trust, meaning, community, and a sense of ownership.

Notes

1. Stephen R. Covey, *Seven Habits of Highly Effective People: Powerful Lessons in Personal Change* (New York: Fireside, 1990), p. 161.

2. Ibid., p. 302.

3. Robert S. Kaplan and David P. Norton, *The Balanced Scorecard: Translating Strategy into Action* (Boston: Harvard Business School Press, 1996).

4. James C. Collins and Jerry I. Porras, *Built to Last: Successful Habits of Visionary Companies* (New York: HarperCollins, 1994).

5. Ibid., p. 55.

6. I would not describe all 18 companies in Collins and Porras's research as visionary. They are basically long-lasting companies that from time to time have shown visionary qualities.

7. Ibid., p. 4.

8. Long-lasting successful companies referred to in *Built to Last*: 3M*, American Express, Boeing, Citicorp, Ford, General Electric, Hewlett-Packard*, IBM*, Johnson & Johnson*, Marriott, Merck*, Motorola*, Nordstrom*, Philip Morris, Procter & Gamble*, Sony, Wal-Mart*, Walt Disney. Companies with * are also listed in the *100 Best Companies to Work for in America*.

9. Comparison companies referred to in *Built to Last*: Norton, Wells Fargo, McDonnell Douglas, Chase Manhattan, GM, Westinghouse, Burroughs, Bristol-Myers Squibb, Howard Johnson, Pfizer, Zenith, Melville, RJR Nabisco, Colgate, Kenwood, Ames, Columbia.

10. Ibid., p. 48.

11. Ibid., p. 57.

12. Ibid., p. 57.

8

Trust, Meaning, Community, and Ownership

At LifeUSA, our employees have options on 2 million shares of company stock. It seems like common sense to us. So why is it still so uncommon in most companies? Sharing the wealth with everyone creates a vested interest for everyone to succeed. It's also a powerful mechanism for accountability. And it encourages people to innovate and provide unbeatable service. Nobody wins unless everyone wins.

—MAGGIE HUGHES, PRESIDENT AND CEO, LIFEUSA HOLDING, INC.

Be wary of the goal of "teams" per se. You may instead want to promote a sense of community in which people are still encouraged to excel as individuals, but do so in a way that promotes a win for themselves and the organization as a whole.

—PETER SCOTT-MORGAN, *THE UNWRITTEN RULES OF THE GAME*

Excessive competitiveness and emphasis on individual performance have eroded the sense of community as individuals compete fiercely for advancement or recognition.

—JOHN W. GARDNER, STANFORD BUSINESS SCHOOL

Organizations build human capital by caring for the physical, emotional, mental, and spiritual needs of their employees. They do this by helping them find personal fulfillment. Employees are motivated by work that gives their lives meaning. When they can see that their efforts are making a difference through service to internal and external customers and society at large, they tap into their highest levels of productivity and creativity. Cultures that release this level of commitment are firmly based in the upper levels of corporate consciousness. They are built around shared values. When a group of people operate with a set of shared values, they create a sense of community. When they live those values, they create a culture of trust.

A CULTURE OF TRUST

Trust is built when people hold common values. Individuals who share a culture—even a low-trust culture—tend to trust each other more than individuals from other cultures. Have you ever noticed when you are traveling abroad how quickly you build bonds with someone from your own country? We do this because we believe that, being from the same culture, the other person shares our values and therefore can be trusted. If we were to meet the same person in our home town, we might not even give them the time of day. The difference in behavior has to do with safety. In a foreign land, we feel uneasy and out of place because we are not part of the culture. In such situations we create bonds with compatriots who we believe share the same values because it increases our sense of safety. It is exactly the same in organizations; when you feel you share the same values as your organization, you begin to trust the organization because you feel safe. With a shared set of positive values you are willing to put your heart and soul into your work because you and your organization care about the same things.

The same thing happens in strong families and strong communities. The trust level is such that people support each other through thick and thin, they make sacrifices to help each other, they empower each other, they take care of their shared environment, and they trust one another with money and emotions. Family and community life is built around values that support the good of the whole. When people go to their place of work, they search for this same set of values. They are often disappointed.

This mismatch of personal and corporate values is perhaps the most pervasive problem facing companies today. To be successful in organizations that focus on self-interest, you have to compromise your personal values and you have to learn to live in a climate of fear. Because there is no trust, there is very little participation and empowerment. No one feels safe.

In such organizations it is easy to lose your family values. You learn to do what is expected of you because that is the only way you can satisfy your physical and emotional needs. Even though we may all have the higher values at our core, we are often prepared to sacrifice them for the sake of security and the respect of our peers. The extent to which we are prepared to do this is illustrated by the research of Amitai Etzioni, professor of sociology at George Washington University. He found that during the period 1976–86, roughly two-thirds of America's 500 largest corporations were involved, to varying degrees, in some form of illegal behavior.[1] The rationales people used to condone this behavior were four: the company will protect me, it is in my or the company's best interest, it is safe because no one will ever find out, or it is not "really" illegal or immoral. At the heart of these rationalizations lies the dilemma of self-interest over the common good.

Making value choices is difficult. It is also uncomfortable, especially when the choices are between lower and higher values—between values that support our physical and emotional needs and values that support our spiritual needs. This is a dilemma we frequently face at work. We know that what is being said or done goes against our higher values, but we feel powerless to stop it. The choice is simple—speak up and risk losing your job or an important promotion, or suffer in silence. This unnatural tension will eventually separate you from your soul. It is fundamentally impossible to spend your life living by two sets of disparate values and not be affected emotionally and physically. The conflict we face is whether to satisfy the needs of the ego (security, relationship, self-esteem) or the needs of the soul (honesty, truth, integrity).

The result of attempting to live in this tension of family and corporate values is frustration and anger. When the things you value are not valued by those with whom you work, you tend to detach. The reason you detach is that your identity is at stake. Whatever we identify with, we care for. When we find ourselves working for an organization that does not live up to our values, then we have difficulty identifying with it. We find it impossible to care for the organization, because it doesn't care for us. Our work becomes a job—something we do from nine to five, to earn a living. Our heart is not in it because who we are is not valued. When we put up with this situation for a long period of time, we become depressed. Depression is anger turned inward. In other words, the frustration we feel about not being able to be our true self, because we are afraid to speak out, turns inward. Depression occurs when there is a lack of alignment between the values of the ego (self-interest) and the values of the soul (common good). If people are to go to work whole, the culture of the organization must be built on a bedrock of trust.

Robert Levering, coauthor of *The 100 Best Companies to Work for in America*, considers trust to be such a significant factor in creating a great place to work that he has created a Trust Index. The index measures the trust employees have in their employers. His survey, consisting of 50 questions, is divided into five dimensions: Credibility, Respect, Fairness, Pride, and Camaraderie—all values that are in the upper levels of consciousness. The survey asks respondents to rate the company as a whole and their smaller work groups on a five-point scale according to such statements as *"Management trusts people to do a good job without looking over their shoulder."* [2]

Jack R. Gibb, author of *Trust: A New View of Personal and Organizational Development*,[3] believes that the level of trust can be used as a barometer of individual and group health. The higher the trust level relative to the fear level, the more effective is the environment for enhancing productivity, creativity, community spirit, and personal growth. As trust declines, our capacity to be open and honest decreases. We become increasingly reliant on rules, contracts, and the law. At the same time, fear

and separation increase. We create boundaries to defend ourselves and hold back from giving our whole self in case our fears
are realized. In the process we become increasingly insular and
isolated. This can be particularly damaging to the productivity
of organizations.

The issue of trust, or more precisely the lack of trust, lies at
the very heart of the difficulty that organizations have in mining
the creative potential of their employees. Ill-managed reengineering and downsizing created cultures of fear. By focusing uniquely on corporate fitness (productivity and efficiency) to improve
corporate survival, organizations have ignored their most important requirement for success—the trust of employees.

For trust to blossom and flourish, there must be shared values and mutual accountability, nurtured by cooperation and
friendship. Above all, there must be a strong sense of working
together for the good of the whole. Therefore, to grow trust, an
organization must first grow community. The foundation of community is sociability (measure of sincere friendliness among
members of community) and solidarity (measure of a community's ability to pursue shared objectives quickly and effectively
regardless of personal ties).[4] When sociability and solidarity are
low, there is little trust, and self-interest predominates. When
sociability and solidarity are high, trust is strong, and the community acts in unity. When a high-trust community is threatened,
it draws closely together to survive. When a low-trust community is threatened, everyone grabs the nearest life belt and looks
after him- or herself. In a world of growing competition, it is clear
that organizations with a strong sense of community will be the
ones who will best survive.

Francis Fukuyama, author of *Trust: The Social Virtues and the
Creation of Prosperity,*[5] concludes that "one of the most important
lessons we can learn from an examination of economic life is that
a nation's well-being, as well as its ability to compete, is conditioned by a single pervasive cultural characteristic: the level of
trust inherent in society." It is not difficult to see that this applies
equally to corporate cultures.

A CULTURE OF MEANING

We find meaning in life when we are able to express our deepest passions and creativity through our work. I am speaking of the work that chooses us. When we are paid to do what we love, we come to work with joy each day. In this situation, we do not need external motivation. Our motivation is internal. When we are fortunate enough to work for a company that understands the importance of aligning people's work with their inner motivation, we are well on the road to finding personal fulfillment.

When we are unable to do the work that gives our life meaning (spiritual motivation), then our motivation must be found in physical, emotional, or mental rewards. We become externally motivated. Internally motivated employees are more productive, creative, and willing to go the extra mile than those who are externally motivated. External motivation is created by incentives that give people the things they desire if they meet certain performance criteria. An example of such a motivation is the promise by Levi Strauss in June 1996 to give its 37,600 worldwide workers an extra year's pay if the company meets a cash flow target of $7.6 billion by 2001. The company estimates that this one-time cash program will cost $750 million.[6] This type of incentive has an appeal to all workers because it addresses our basic need for financial security. However, it does very little to satisfy workers' internal motivations.

Alfie Kohn, author of five books dealing with motivation, believes that reward systems are tantamount to manipulation or "control through seduction." Eventually people react against this type of control. He states, "I uncovered a huge amount of data in the 80's that suggests that competition substantially reduces the quality of work or learning that people are engaged in as well as undermining relationship and psychological health."[7] The context for internal motivation is destroyed when individuals or teams compete for rewards.

Discovering your inner motivation is part of the process of self-actualization. In the words of Henrik Ibsen, the Norwegian playwright, each person is born with "sealed marching orders.

But when they are opened, they all say the same thing: You are here in this world to realize yourself."[8] Each of us has a special gift to give, but we must first discover it. The process of discovering the gift takes place during transformation. In *"A Guide to Liberating Your Soul,"* I describe the gift in the following way: "Every soul brings a unique gift. The [gift] is often called the soul's purpose. The scope of the purpose may be large or small; it may involve supporting another human being, or assisting thousands. Whatever it is, it will involve some form of service to the human race or planet Earth. You may not be specifically aware of your soul's purpose, but you will probably recognize that there are certain activities from which you derive immense satisfaction. If you want to find out your soul's purpose, search out those experiences that give you *the most* satisfaction. Whatever it is that gives you an inner sense of meaning will be closely linked to your soul's purpose. Very often we know our soul's purpose, but do not want to acknowledge it. This is because it does not correspond with our chosen career, or the identity we have carefully cultivated for ourselves. For those well established in their careers, the pathway to soul consciousness can sometimes mean making painful choices. You may feel the need to give up your career and start anew. The form and size of the gift you bring is not important. What is important is that you give your gift unconditionally. The offering of this gift is the service you bring to humanity."[9]

Finding your soul purpose, and living it out, is the greatest gift you can give yourself. Choosing to follow your passion floods your life with meaning. Once you discover this new way of being, you become totally self-motivated. You no longer have a career. Your work becomes your mission. There is nothing else for you to do. You never retire from your mission; once you have discovered it, it is with you always. You are able to tap into your creativity through your intuition—the knowledge of the soul. When you listen to your intuition and commit to fulfilling your purpose, you unleash creative and synchronistic energies that move you forward. The following quotation captures this concept in a splendid way: "Concerning all acts of initiative (and creation) there is one elementary truth, the ignorance of which kills countless ideas and splendid plans: that the moment one definitely commits oneself, then Providence moves too. All sorts of things occur to help one that would never otherwise have occurred. A whole stream of events issues from the decision, raising in one's favor all manner of unforeseen incidents and meetings and material assistance, which no [human] could have dreamed would have come his way."[10]

I can attest, from many years of experience, to the truth of this statement. So much so that I learned to eliminate the word "impossible" from my life. Once you commit to your mission, all manner of synchronistic circumstances move you forward. The recognition of this unseen support brings a deep sense of meaning and connectedness to life. Kahlil Gibran, who wrote *The Prophet*, summarized it beautifully when he wrote, *"Work is love made visible."*

Richard McKnight, an organizational psychologist, believes that having a transcendent purpose "results in being in love with the world" and allows integration and direction in your life and work.[11] He says, "People have needs in three areas: body, mind, and spirit. Yet most companies, if they acknowledge that people have needs at all, act as if there are only two requirements for producing good work: money and job security."[12] His experience reveals that most workers suffer from one of two spiritual syndromes at work: "Either they are devoted only to non-transcendent materialistic purposes such as career advancement [lower needs]; or they have a transcendent purpose that doesn't mesh with the purpose of the company."[13]

The challenge for organizations in the twenty-first century is to create a work environment that encourages personal fulfillment—taking care of employees' physical, emotional, mental, and spiritual needs. It also means providing opportunities for workers to live out their passions and providing opportunities for service. In one survey it was discovered that nearly half of all Americans would be more satisfied with their lives if they felt they could do more to make a difference in their community.[14]

In November 1995, a *Newsweek* poll reported that 58% of Americans feel the need to experience spiritual growth. The quest of these seekers is to find meaning. What better place to

find meaning than through your work? The problem that arises is that when we attempt to bring our search for meaning into
the workplace it is rarely appreciated. The reason—the majority of our organizations operate from the lower levels of consciousness. They are stuck in the values of survival, relationship, or self-esteem consciousness. The only way forward is
transformation.

A CULTURE OF COMMUNITY

How do we create an organizational culture, based on trust and
meaning? By creating a true sense of community. In *Community
Building: Renewing Spirit and Learning in Business*, Scott Peck states:
"Community in the workplace is not some airy-fairy, impossible
ideal. It does require considerably more sustained psychospiritu-
al exertion from the top management on down than does 'business as usual.' On the other hand, it will also make most work,
from top management on down, ultimately more satisfying and
fulfilling, more creative and productive, more profitable and cost
effective."[15]

Community building is a journey to wholeness.[16] It is about
creating the conditions that support sociability (sincere friendliness) and solidarity (ability to pursue shared objectives quickly
and efficiently). We create sociability in an organization by building relationships based on trust. We create solidarity in an organization by uniting behind a common purpose. When individuals
wholeheartedly support a common purpose, they forget their differences. When the purpose is to be successful in business, having
a common purpose is not enough; solidarity will be achieved only
when the common purpose yields benefits that are shared by all
the community.

Another key element in creating solidarity is the elimina-
tion of boundaries. Wherever there are boundaries in organizations you find organizational subcultures that can undermine the
common good. In the *Boundaryless Organization*,[17] the authors
identify four types of boundaries: *vertical*—those based on hierarchy that differentiate status, authority, and power (floors and

ceilings); *horizontal*—those based on functions, product lines, or units (walls between rooms); *external*—those based on a separate organizational identity such as suppliers, customers, government agencies, special interest groups, or community organizations; and *geographic*—those based on location when large companies operate in different markets and countries.

In organizations with fewer vertical boundaries less attention is given to who has authority or rank and more is given to who has useful ideas. Rank is less relevant than competence. In organizations with fewer horizontal boundaries less attention is given to internal transactions and more is given to serving the needs of clients. Customers are concerned about the quality, speed, and cost of products and services. Horizontal boundaries slow down processes and compartmentalize operations, creating opportunities for internal self-interest to take priority over customer satisfaction. In organizations with fewer external boundaries, customers and suppliers play a role in improving effectiveness and products. The focus is on the confluence of interests and what is best for the common good. Less time and effort are wasted on haggling, negotiating, manipulation, politics, and withholding information.

The authors of *The Boundaryless Organization* conclude that: "When vertical, horizontal, external, and geographic boundaries are traversable, the organization of the future begins to take shape. When these four boundaries remain rigid and impenetrable—as they do in many organizations today—they create the slowness to respond and the lack of flexibility and innovation that causes premier companies to fail."[18]

The greatest danger of boundaries in organizations is the opportunity they provide for the development of *us and them* cultures—the creation of separation based on culturally reinforced identities. The idea of an elite group that basks in status and privileges is an anathema to creating a true community. Companies are overcoming this issue by referring to everyone as an associate, flattening hierarchical structures and doing away with status symbols.

Equally important to eliminating management/staff boundaries is the need to eradicate the boundaries of gender and race. Why is this important other than on moral grounds? Organizations are finding that diversity gives them a competitive advantage. The ability to tap into the thoughts and ideas of different belief systems and life experiences provides a wellspring of knowledge that feeds creativity and innovation. However, this advantage emerges only when participation is present.

According to the research of Carolyn Schaffer and Kristin Anundsen, "Community is a dynamic whole that emerges when a group of people:

- Participate in common practices
- Depend on one another
- Make decisions together
- Identify themselves as part of something larger than the sum of their individual relationships; and Commit themselves for the long term to their own, one another's and the group's well-being."[19]

In *A World Waiting to Be Born: Civility Rediscovered*, Scott Peck defines community as "a way of being together with both individual authenticity and interpersonal harmony so that people become able to function with a collective energy even greater than the sum of their individual energies."[20]

As I have already mentioned, creating a unifying vision with a "higher" purpose is an essential component of community building. But it is not enough. The organization must also adhere to and support behaviors that create a sense of community. Above all, this means the active participation of employees, customers, suppliers, and community groups in the affairs of the organization. Participation is the consummate tool for breaking down the barriers of *us and them*.

Patricia McLagan and Christo Nel in *The Age of Participation* state that "The shift to participatory governance in the workplace is both inevitable and necessary."[21] Participatory governance is inevitable, first, because it is one of the defining characteristics of the stage of evolution of global consciousness that we have now entered, and second, because that is what the most successful companies will be doing in the twenty-first century—it will become one of the key factors in providing competitive advantage. Organizations that do not develop participatory cultures will be hard pressed to survive in the twenty-first century.

Moral democracy and economic democracy are essential components of a culture that nurtures community. This calls for transparent forms of governance in which workers are encouraged to fulfill their potential and make contributions that affect the good of the whole. The shift to empowering, participation-based, structures from autocratic, control-based structures requires a commitment to community.

Not only is the baby boomer generation demanding this change, so are young people. Claire Raines, coauthor of *Twenty-something: Managing & Motivating Today's New Work Force*, states that young people are drawn to the idea of community—the idea of fellowship and mutual striving and alignment around a common, worthwhile goal.[22] Ron Zemke, senior editor of *Training* magazine, believes that the longing for community is based on "a desire to create a life that works—a life that focuses more on meaning and growth, less on career, standard of living and financial reward."

A CULTURE OF OWNERSHIP

Communities work best when there are psychological and financial ownership and transparency of governance. Organizations create psychological ownership through participation, they create financial ownership through stock ownership programs and they create transparency of governance through open-book management.

Employees develop psychological ownership when they are invited to participate in decision making. Participation opens up avenues for employees to address their *mental* need to grow and develop and their *spiritual* need to find meaning, make a difference, and be of service. The sense of ownership is heightened when employees are also given a financial stake in the organization that satisfies their need for long-term physical security.

A five-year study involving in-depth case studies of employee ownership companies by the National Center for Employee Ownership in Oakland showed that over a 10-year period companies with employee stock ownership schemes (ESOPs) grew 40 to 60 percent faster than they would have done without the ESOP. Most of the growth, however, was accounted for by the minority of companies that practiced employee involvement. The most participative companies grew 11 to 17 percent faster than the least participative companies. The least participative companies did worse after their ESOP was established than they did before.[23]

Stock ownership gives employees a long-term stake in the success of the company, but if they are unable to contribute their ideas, then that stake is really nothing more than an inferior pension plan—the stock of the company could go up, but it could also go down. In situations in which there is financial ownership but no participation, employees feel that they have little control over the outcome of the company and therefore are not psychologically engaged. The research clearly shows that the impact of ESOPs on their own is limited. Only when they are implemented in combination with participative management do they create high-performance organizations.

Whereas there has been little research on the impact of stock options, the research on ESOPs (which function more like retirement plans) is quite conclusive.[24] It consistently shows that broad employee ownership can have a significant effect on the bottom line, but only if there is a culture in which employees are trained and encouraged to act like owners.[25] Becoming an owner means having full information on goals and performance and transparency of governance. The process of open-book management provides a proven technique for making this happen.

The concept of open-book management is simple. When you teach employees the basics of business, trust them to make good decisions based on knowledge, and treat them as responsible stakeholders, they will make significant contributions to the organization's success.[26] Open-book management is basically an institutionalized form of participation in which every individual in the organization is required to become a responsible member of the community. To assist them in that objective, they are trained in understanding and interpreting the organization's performance goals.

In values-driven organizations, where success is measured against a broad range of performance measures, the practice of open-book management requires employees to become familiar with the organization's Balanced Needs Scorecard goals, objectives, and performance measures. All employees should know how they individually contribute to the success of the organization and be able to trace the impact of their performance to at least one of the Balance Needs Scorecard goals. Apart from the benefit of increased innovation through institutionalized participation, open-book management also helps to build a strong sense of community through shared knowledge and mutual accountability.

Building an organizational culture that honors higher level values such as trust, meaning, community, and ownership requires leaders who are themselves focused in the higher levels of consciousness. The next chapter describes the type of leadership that is necessary to create a long-lasting, values-driven organization.

Notes

1. Saul W. Gellerman, "Why 'good' managers make bad ethical choices," *Harvard Business Review*, July–August 1986, p. 85.

2. Eric Matson, "Trust! (but verify)," *Fast Company Magazine*, April/May, 1996, p. 52.

3. Jack R. Gibb, *Trust: A New View of Personal and Organizational Development* (The Guild of Tutors Press, 1978).

4. Rob Goffee and Gareth Jones, "What holds the modern company together?" *Harvard Business Review*, November–December 1996, pp. 133–148.

5. Francis Fukuyama, *Trust: The Social Virtues and the Creation of Prosperity* (New York: Free Press, 1996), p. 7.

6. "Extra cash in their jeans?" *The Washington Post*, Business Section, June 13, 1996.

7. Alfie Kohn, "How incentives undermine performance," *Journal of Quality and Participation*, March/April 1998, pp. 7–13.

8. Quoted by Tor Dahl in *Perspectives on Business and Global Change*, Vol. 10, No. 4, World Business Academy, A New Look at High Performance, Interview with Tor Dahl, p. 21.

9. Richard Barrett, *A Guide to Liberating Your Soul* (Alexandria: Fulfilling Books, 1995), p. 98.

10. Goethe, "Until one is committed," in Robert Bly et al., *The Rag and Bone Shop of the Heart: Poems for Men* (New York: HarperCollins, 1992), p. 235.

11. Mathew Fox, *The Reinvention of Work: A New Vision of Livelihood for Our Time* (New York: HarperCollins), p. 237.

12. Richard McKnight, "Spirituality in the workplace," in *Transforming Work*, ed. John D. Adams (Alexandria, VA: Miles River Press, 1984), p. 142.

13. Ibid. p. 145.

14. Ibid.

15. Scott Peck, *Community Building: Renewing Spirit and Learning in Business* (San Francisco: Sterling & Stone, Inc., 1995), p. 6.

16. Ibid., p. 415 (Conclusion: Hope for Closing the Gap by Kazimeirz Gozdz).

17. Ron Ashkenas, Dave Ulrich, Todd Jick, and Steve Kerr, *The Boundaryless Organization: Breaking the Chains of Organizational Structure* (San Francisco: Jossey-Bass, 1995), pp. 11–13.

18. Ibid., p. 13.

19. Ron Zemke, "The Call of Community," *Training*, March 1996, p. 27.

20. Ibid., p. 27. Quoted from Scott Peck's *A World Waiting to Be Born: Civility Rediscovered*.

21. Patricia McLagan and Christo Nel, *The Age of Participation* (San Francisco: Berrett-Koehler, 1995). Quotation taken from, Vol. 10, No. 1 (World Business Academy, 1996).

22. Ron Zemke, "The Call of Community," *Training*, March 1996, pp. 24–25.

23. Karen M. Young, "Success Through Participation," *At Work*, May/June, 1994, Berrett-Koehler, San Francisco.

24. Ibid.

25. Ibid.

26. P. N. Schuster, J. Carpenter, and M. P. Kane, *The Power of Open-Book Management* (New York: John Wiley & Sons, 1996).

9

Seven Levels of Leadership Consciousness

If our economic organizations are going to live up to their potential, we must find, develop, and encourage more people to lead in the service of others. Without leadership, firms cannot adapt to a fast moving world. But if leaders do not have the hearts of servants, there is only the potential for tyranny.

> —JOHN P. KOTTER AND JAMES L. HESKETT, HARVARD BUSINESS SCHOOL

I try to remember that people—good, intelligent, capable people—may actually need day-to-day praise and thanks for the job they do. I try to remember to get up out of my chair, turn off my computer, go sit or stand next to them and see what they're doing, ask about the challenges, find out if they need additional help, offer that help if possible, and most of all, tell them in all honesty that what they are doing is important: to me, to the company, and to our customers.

> —JOHN BALL, SERVICE TRAINING MANAGER, AMERICAN HONDA COMPANY

I don't know what your destiny will be, but one thing I do know; the only ones among you who will be really happy are those who have sought and found how to serve.

> —ALBERT SCHWEITZER

The core of leadership is vision. Vision is seeing the potential purpose hidden in the chaos of the moment, but which could bring to birth new possibilities for a person, a company, or a nation.

> —WILLIAM VAN DUSEN WISHARD

DEFINING A LEADER

The future well-being of the humanity currently rests in the hands of the leaders of business. Collectively, they wield more power for good or evil than do our political leaders. If we are to overcome the global crises that I described in Chapter 2, then there needs to be an increase in the number of leaders throughout the world who are grounded in the consciousness of the common good. This chapter and the next are devoted to identifying the characteristics of such leaders and the type of training necessary to build leaders who can fulfill this role. Let us begin by examining the following definition of a leader:

> "Leader" is a label we give to an individual who holds a vision and courageously pursues that vision in such a way that it resonates with the psyche of people.

According to this definition, being a leader has nothing to do with the formal title that one might hold in an organizational hierarchy. To earn the title of leader you must stand for something that *resonates* in the minds or hearts of people. It is the resonance with the leader's message that causes people to follow. People support a leader because they feel the leader is speaking for them. He or she is articulating in words and actions what they feel inside. It is the leader's message that inspires people. Based on the preceding definition, we can identify three characteristics of leaders: they hold a vision, the vision resonates with people, and they are fearless in pursuing their vision.

This definition applies to highly acclaimed leaders such as Jesus Christ and infamous leaders such as Adolf Hitler. They were both leaders who courageously held a vision that resonated with the psyche of the people they led. The difference is that in one case the resonance was based on love and in the other case it was based on fear. The appeal of Christ's message was that it resonated with people's higher values. Hitler's message, on the other hand, resonated with the German people's need for a stronger collective self-esteem. At that time in history, they needed to believe in the supremacy of the Aryan race. The stature of Hitler as a leader was short lived, whereas the stature of Christ as a leader continues to this day. To understand the difference between resonance of love and the resonance of fear, we need to delve into the workings of the human mind.

The human psyche is composed of two poles. At one end of the continuum lies the ego and at the other lies the soul. The ego is the aspect of our psyche that sees itself as physical and separate and acts as the repository of all our fears. The soul is the aspect of the psyche that sees itself as spiritual and connected and the repository of all our love. The ego uses the mind to rationalize its actions. The soul works through the heart and in any particularly circumstance knows what to do. The soul never imposes itself on the ego. It waits patiently to be invited to present its point of view.

Our personalities lie somewhere on the continuum between the ego and the soul. They display a mixture of values, some of which emanate from the fears of the ego and some of which emanate from the love of the soul. When an individual is motivated by fear, the personality is reflecting the concerns of the ego. When an individual is motivated by love, the personality is reflecting the concerns of the soul. We grow closer to our soul when we are able to face our fears and embrace truth and love. When we are unable to face our fears, we choose safety over growth. The personality moves closer to the ego and away from the soul. Thus, Hitler was a leader whose message resonated with the concerns of the egos of the German people. Christ was a leader whose message resonated with the concerns of the souls of the early Christians. With this understanding of the difference between the ego and the soul, let us be more specific in our definition of the type of leader that is necessary at this critical time in the evolution of the human race.

A leader is someone who holds a vision and courageously pursues that vision in such a way that it resonates with the *souls* of people.

Thus, when we speak of liberating the corporate soul we are talking about creating a corporate culture that resonates with the values that are held in the souls of employees. These are the values that correspond to the upper three levels of human consciousness. The benefits that accompany liberating the corporate soul include increased integrity, honesty, trust, commitment, responsibility, accountability, productivity, innovation and creativity, access to the intuition, strategic alliances with customers and suppliers, and the loyalty and goodwill of employees, the local community, and society at large. Such cultures can be created only by leaders who have moved beyond transformation to embrace the values of the fifth, sixth, and seventh levels of human consciousness. Why? Because whatever values leaders hold have an impact on the organizational culture.

Let us now define, based on the seven levels of human consciousness, the seven levels of leadership consciousness. This will help us understand the essential differences between a manager and a leader and the qualities that we need to develop in our leaders if we are to survive on this planet through the twenty-first century.

THE SEVEN LEVELS OF LEADERSHIP

The Seven Levels of Human Consciousness translate directly into Seven Levels of Leadership Consciousness. The principal focus of the lower three levels of consciousness is self-interest and the principal focus of the upper three levels of consciousness is the common good. The focus of the middle level is transformation. The following distinctions between the different levels of leadership draw on the work of Brian Hall,[1] Robert Quinn,[2] and Robert Greenleaf.[3]

Authoritarian

Authoritarians are strongly motivated by the need to control. They use a dictatorial style to get what they want because they find it difficult to relate to people in an open and caring way. They are afraid of their emotions. They don't ask. They give orders. They are afraid to let go of the reins of power because they have great difficulty in trusting others. The greater their fears, the more risk averse they become. They are quick to anger and feel uncomfortable discussing emotions. If they have insecurities about money, they will exploit others for their own ends.

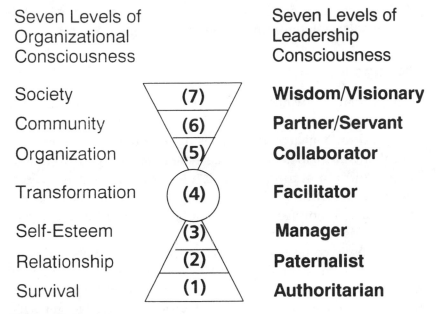

Seven Levels of Organizational Consciousness		Seven Levels of Leadership Consciousness
Society	(7)	**Wisdom/Visionary**
Community	(6)	**Partner/Servant**
Organization	(5)	**Collaborator**
Transformation	(4)	**Facilitator**
Self-Esteem	(3)	**Manager**
Relationship	(2)	**Paternalist**
Survival	(1)	**Authoritarian**

Figure 9–1
Seven Levels of Leadership Consciousness

Authoritarians can create emotionally unhealthy climates in which to work.

Paternalist

Paternalists are motivated by the need to form relationships. They are basically authoritarians who need to be liked. Unfortunately, their need to be liked cannot overcome their need to control. So they become benevolent dictators. They are protective of their people but demand loyalty, discipline, and obedience in return. They will ask you your opinion in order to make you feel that they care but will go ahead and do what they want anyway. In this sense they are manipulative. The fears of paternalists are such that they find it very difficult to trust others. This type of consciousness often shows up in family-run businesses. Anyone outside the family is not to be trusted. This severely limits the pool of talent that the organization can draw on. Paternalists create environments that kill the entrepreneurial spirit of employees.

Manager

Managers are motivated by the need for order and respect. They regard what they do as a science. They enjoy structure, measurement, and rational analysis. Exercising their intellect has a strong appeal. Inwardly focused managers are good at organizing information and monitoring results. Outwardly focused managers anticipate work flow problems and get things done. They are productive and accomplish goals. They plan and prioritize their work and provide stability and continuity. They create schedules and enjoy being in control. They focus on training for skills and want to learn the latest management techniques. When managers' needs for respect are driven by subconscious fear, they are ambitious and competitive. They will play office politics to get what they want and they will avoid giving their boss bad news. Their need for order can get them stuck in the status quo. Their need for rewards can lead them to work long hours and neglect their families. Managers create environments that are productive and efficient but can be very demanding if they are not balanced.

Facilitator

Facilitators are in transition. They are learning to release their fears so that they can move from being outer directed (satisfying the needs of the ego) to being inner directed (satisfying the needs of the soul). They are in the process of self-actualization. As they let go of their need for outer approval, they begin to discover who they really are. As they let go of their need to control, they invite participation and consensus building. They become enablers— helping others to express themselves. They are no longer wedded to their careers. Now they want to develop their vision and work on their mission. They want work that aligns with their inner passion, and they want to learn about themselves through training that focuses on personal growth. They become more open and innovative and begin to search for balance in their lives. Balance leads to detachment and independence and allows them to become objective about their strengths and weaknesses. They focus on interpersonal communication skills, conflict resolution, and team building. Facilitators are in the process of shifting from being a manager to being a leader.

Collaborator

Collaborators are motivated by the need to find meaning. One of the ways they find meaning is through creating community. They are engineers of human capital and they build trust. They are more concerned about getting the best result for everyone than for their own self-interest. They are flexible and adaptive and focused on values. They walk their talk. They are creative problem solvers. They recognize that they don't have to have all the answers. They are willing to be vulnerable. They are honest and truthful and are willing to confront people and their bosses because they have little fear. They feel confident in handling any situation. This confidence and openness allow them to reclassify problems as opportunities. They are authentic, democratic and enthusiastic. They are intuitive and creative. They clarify priorities, communicate vision, and plan for the long term. They display emotional as well as intellectual intelligence. Collaborators are good at bringing out the best in their people.

Servant/Partner

Servant/partners are motivated by the need to make a difference and be of service to those whom they lead. They serve the organization by creating partnerships and strategic alliances with external organizations. At the same time, they care for their people, seeking ways to ensure that employees find personal fulfillment through their work. They view situations from a systems perspective, seeing beyond the narrow boundaries of cause and effect. They build systems that support employees, and they seek to form mutually beneficial alliances with suppliers and customers. They are active in the local community, building relationships that create goodwill. They recognize the importance of environmental and social stewardship and will go beyond the letter of the law in making their operations environmentally friendly. They are empathetic and careful listeners. They are also mentors and coaches. Servant/partners create supportive internal and external linkages that build commitment and goodwill.

Wisdom/Visionary

Wisdom/visionary leaders are motivated by the need to be of service to the world. They are constantly asking, "How can I help?" Their vision is global. They see their own mission and that of their organization from a societal perspective. For them the world is a complex web of interconnectedness, and they know they have an important role to play. They play their role with humility. They are generous, forgiving, and compassionate and able to relate to people at all levels. They are concerned about the state of the world—peace, justice, ethics, and ecology—and they are concerned for future generations. They are not prepared to compromise long-term outcomes for short-term gains. They enjoy solitude and are at ease with uncertainty. Visionary leaders are admired for their wisdom, vision, and commitment to ethics.

Every individual, like every organization, is distributed across the seven levels of consciousness. No one is ever focused uniquely at one level. The values of most leaders are clustered around two or three adjacent levels of higher consciousness. Sometimes they hold organizational values that are situated in the higher levels of consciousness but may have many deeply ingrained personal fears about being liked or respected. Such individuals may form wonderful strategic alliances with external partners, but they are terribly demanding and unsympathetic to their direct staff.

LEADERS OR MANAGERS?

According to my definition, those who are in positions of authority but primarily display values that are focused in the lower three levels of consciousness are not leaders. They are, at best, managers. Their actions and behaviors are mainly directed by the fears of the ego rather than the love of the soul. They are motivated by their conscious and subconscious fears. They tend to operate with values and behaviors that play it safe, please others, or achieve recognition or respect. Only when they become inner directed and have emerged from transformation are they able to overcome the power of their subconscious fears.

According to John Gardener, professor at Stanford Business School, leaders distinguish themselves from managers in the following ways: they think long-term; they see the big picture and the interconnections (global systems perspective); they reach and influence people beyond their normal jurisdictions; they place heavy emphasis on vision, values, and motivation; they are politically adept; and they constantly think in terms of renewal. Above all, leaders show strong emotional intelligence—they know how to empower people to reach their individual and collective dreams. And when the people have attained their dreams, they are able to say, *"We did it ourselves."*

This is the type of leader that is in short supply in corporate America today. According to a 1997 survey of 9,144 workers carried out by Watson Wyatt consultants at large and small companies across the country, fewer than half of the workers thought their supervisors dealt fairly with them, clearly communicated goals, built teamwork, or were able to coach workers to greater success. Only 36 percent of workers reported that their companies actively sought worker's opinions and suggestions. Despite the grievances with their bosses and organizations, 61 percent of workers liked their jobs. Research involving over 25,000 workers by the Wilson Learning Corporation shows that an employee's relationship to her or his superior has a critical impact on performance. Almost 69 percent of the variability in employee satisfaction is attributable to the actions of the work unit leader, and over

39 percent of the variability in organizational performance is attributable to work unit satisfaction. The only way an organization can tap into the intellectual capital of its employees is to develop a cadre of leaders, managers, and supervisors who display emotional intelligence.[4]

Although "bad" bosses still outnumber "enlightened leaders," there is a growing trend toward hiring CEOs with "feel-good" people skills. The recent search for a new leader at Delta Airlines specified that the leader should be "a great listener and capture the imagination of Delta employees."[5]

Howard Gardner, professor of education at the Harvard Graduate School, believes that leaders "exercise their influence through their stories or messages, *and* through the traits that they embody."[6] When the messages they give and the traits they embody are inconsistent, they cannot truly be called leaders. All leaders worthy of being called leaders walk their talk. Mahatma Ghandi put it very succinctly when he said, *"My life is my message."* A question we should all frequently ask ourselves is, "Is my life my message?" And if it isn't, "Why isn't it?"

Making your life your message speaks to the issues of mission and authenticity. True leaders have nothing to hide. There is no falsehood or misrepresentation. Their lives are consistent with their mission and message. Because their values are in alignment with the common good, they are *fear-less*. They are at ease with themselves in any situation, because they have no secrets and nothing to hide. Their defenselessness and unashamed vulnerability make them powerful.

THE NEW LEADERS

In the past decade, as the spotlight of values has turned toward business, we have begun to see the emergence of successful business leaders who embrace the philosophy of the common good. Some focus their attention on building corporate community (level 5 actions); others are developing strategic alliances with customers, suppliers, and the local community (level 6 actions); and some are acting globally to reduce inequality and poverty and defend human rights (level 7 actions). Four such leaders are Tom Chappell, Anita Roddick, J. Irwin Miller, and the Haas family.

Tom Chappell, cofounder and CEO of Tom's of Maine, which produces all-natural personal care products with environmentally sensitive packaging, has tried to instill in his company the *freedom to serve*.[7] For Tom, that is the ultimate freedom. He sees it as a paradox—in using your freedom to serve others, you become bound to them in your shared concern for your good and their good—the common good. Tom believes that "Without this kind of autonomy, there is no morality. Freedom rests at the core of the moral corporation—the freedom to serve others. The business leader who can take the freedom he or she has as the head of a company and transmit it to his executives and employees—integrates it into his business strategy—will have re-imagined the essence of his business. No longer will he be the head of a company managed by fear and second-guessing. Creativity and innovation—freedom's children—will reign."

Anita Roddick, founder and CEO of The Body Shop, has created a worldwide chain of stores that are attempting to integrate social, human, and ecological values into the business of selling skin and hair care products. Employees of The Body Shop are encouraged to be activists for positive social change. Anita has tried to create a company in which people can live out their dreams through business and in which service and making a difference in the local community and the world at large are a way of life. Through her business Anita is not only serving the needs of her own staff to find meaning and purpose but also empowering women in developing countries by buying raw materials from them. "In my company," Anita states, "finding your spirit through service allows us to be conscious participants and practice bringing the power of the inner world into a specific and positive action that can effectively meet human needs."[8]

J. Irwin Miller, general manager, president, and board chairman of Cummins, a worldwide manufacturer of engines, created a highly successful company through implementing the philosophy of the servant-leader. He explains, "A leadership that is concentrated on the ideas of one person is very limited. Genuine leadership involves getting all the wisdom that is available in a group, and helping that group come to a better decision than any one of its members would have been able to achieve himself. The servant-leader is the person who gets the unsuspected best out of his group of people."[9] Miller created an open learning culture that provides a place for people to grow and live as a community. At the core of Miller's management style is "the life long cultivation of the capacity to feel." For Miller, a man is only half-man if he is not in touch with his feelings. Without being able to express his feelings, a worker is "half-happy, half-bored, and half-effective." Miller was also a leader and a supporter of the local community. When someone embezzled money from Irwin Union Bank and Trust, which he inherited from his father, Irwin told the parole board that he would provide a job for the man when he was free.

The Haas family of Levi Strauss & Co. have infused their business with values ever since the company was founded in 1853. From the very beginning the family business gained a reputation for high quality, fair prices, and a strong commitment to the community. The Haas family has always treated their employees with exceptional dignity and respect and has always been at the forefront of social justice. They were among the first companies in the south to desegregate and maintain a strong diversity policy. They created Community Affairs departments in all their facilities to help workers organize themselves into groups of volunteers to work in the local community. They provided start-up money and matching funds for these worker efforts. If an employee has been actively involved in a community organization for one year, the organization receives a donation of $500. If an employee sits on the board of a nonprofit organization, Levi Strauss & Co. donates between $500 and $1,500, depending on the size and budget of the organization. Levi now has more than 100 Community Involvement teams working all over the world. The philosophy of the Haas family when it comes to business is best expressed by the words of Walter **Haas**, Jr. speaking at the 1992 Business Enterprise Awards Ceremony: "Each of us has the capacity to make a business not only a source of economic wealth, but also a force for economic and social justice. Each of us needs to recognize and use the power we have to define the character of our enterprises, so they nurture values important to our society. Only then will each of us know the full rewards that a career in business can yield. Only then will business achieve the true potential of its leadership. Only then will business fulfill its obligation to help build an economy worthy of a free society and a civilization worth celebrating."[10]

These are just a few of several hundred stories. If you want to read more, turn to *The 100 Best Companies to Work for in America*[11] or *Aiming Higher: Twenty-five Stories of How Companies Prosper by Combining Sound Management and Social Vision*.[12] The depth and breadth of corporate caring in values-driven organizations all over North America is inspiring. What is remarkable is that, almost without exception, the companies that are living in this way are amongst the top performers in their sectors.

The challenge that all these organizations face, and every other company that wants to build a values-driven culture faces, is how to transform their managers into leaders. This is the issue that we will address in the following chapter.

Maintaining a values-driven organizational culture requires a shift in emphasis from managership to leadership. It requires people who are authentic, identify with the common good, and are balanced in their approach to life. In short, it requires self-actualized individuals who operate primarily from the higher levels of consciousness. There is no room for self-interest in a values-driven organization. The key issues for leaders of the future will be personal transformation, emotional intelligence, building strategic alliances, and making the organization a responsible member of the local community and a good global citizen.

Notes

1. Brian P. Hall, *Values Shift: A Guide to Personal and Organizational Transformation* (Rockport, MA: Twin Lights, 1994).
2. Robert E. Quinn, *Prism 3: Competing Values Development Tool* (San Francisco: Jossey-Bass, 1992).

3. Robert K. Greenleaf, *Servant Leadership: A Journey into the Nature of Legitimate Power and Greatness* (Mahwah: Paulist Press, 1977).

4. Kirstin Downey Grimsley, "Employees pleased with jobs, not managers, survey finds," *Washington Post*, Business Section, September 2, 1997.

5. Sharon Walsh, "Captains courteous," *Washington Post*, Business Section, August 31, 1997.

6. Howard Gardner, *Leading Minds: An Anatomy of Leadership* (New York: Basic Books, 1996), p. 37.

7. Tom Chappell, *The Soul of a Business: Managing for Profit and the Common Good* (New York: Bantam Books, 1994), p. 159.

8. Anita Roddick, *Finding Spirit Through Service*, contribution to *The New Bottom Line* (San Francisco: New Leaders Press, 1996), p. 328.

9. David Bollier, *Aiming Higher* (New York: AMACOM, 1997), p. 302.

10. Ibid., pp. 339–351.

11. Robert Levering and Milton Moskowitz, *The 100 Best Companies to Work for in America* (New York: Currency Doubleday, 1993).

12. David Bollier, *Aiming Higher: Twenty-five Stories of How Companies Prosper by Combining Sound Management and Social Vision* (New York: AMACOM, 1997).

10

Leadership Development and Assessment

The triumph of the mission—and its joy—is that we are being ourselves in running the business. Our knowledge that our values matter keeps reinforcing our identity, sharpening our competitive edge. Most important we have taken control of our future. [We all need to be able to] lead with who we are, live with who we are, [and] progress according to who we are. But if our souls aren't on the journey, if our quest is only about figuring out another plan, it will be just another strategy, just another plan, just another game. Living and working are too important to let that happen.

— TOM CHAPPELL, COFOUNDER AND CEO OF TOM'S OF MAINE

A financial analyst once asked me if I was afraid of losing control. I told him I've never had control and I never wanted it. If you create an environment where the people truly participate you don't need control. They know what needs to be done, and they do it.

— HERB KELLEHER, CEO OF SOUTHWEST AIRLINES

The good life is to live on honorable terms with your own soul.

— SAUL BELLOW

It's almost axiomatic to say that personal change must precede or at least accompany management and organizational change . . . attempting to change an organization or a management style without first changing one's own habit patterns is analogous to attempting to improve one's tennis game before developing the muscles that make better strokes possible.

— STEPHEN COVEY, PRINCIPLE-CENTERED LEADERSHIP

THREE STAGES OF LEADERSHIP DEVELOPMENT

Most people are conditioned by their parents and teachers to begin their working lives somewhere in the lower three levels of consciousness—seeking security and self-esteem. I know for myself that when I first started work as an engineer I was totally conditioned to getting on in the world. I was stuck in level 3 consciousness. Status and salary meant everything to me. Being successful was all I cared about. By the age of 26, I was running the Paris office of a large UK-based international consulting company. Within three years I had opened a second office in the south of France and we had 18 full-time staff. Everyone thought that I was very successful. Everyone, that is, except me. Inside it felt empty and meaningless. I was managing staff and attempting to bring in new work 12 hours a day and 7 days a week. I was so stressed that the blood vessels in my eyes began to leak.

I returned to the head office of the UK company after four years in France, and two years later I left the company. I became a one-man international consulting firm operating out of rural Somerset. I moved to the countryside to find myself. As I learned how to get in touch with my true self and my inner motivations, I found that my greatest passion was my own creativity. Applying my creativity in service to others was what I loved to do. After a couple of years, the World Bank became my main client and began to monopolize my time. I loved working in developing countries because I felt that I was able to make a difference.

To find real happiness at work, I had learned that I had to stop putting my energy into pleasing my boss, competing with others, and being the best. I had to release my unconscious fears about being valued and respected and pass through transformation. When I was free of the fears that were driving my competitive behavior, I was able to be my true self and be my own person. Only then was I able to discover my true passion and the joy of working in service to others.

Since that time in Paris, over 20 years ago, I have devoted a large part of my energies to understanding the process of personal transformation and how individuals can attain the higher levels of consciousness. My thoughts on this topic are detailed in *A Guide to Liberating Your Soul*.[1] What I discovered is that personal transformation is the gateway to leadership. We are not able to become true leaders until we become authentic individuals, and we are not able to become authentic individuals until we release our unconscious fears. The good news is that there are tools and techniques to assist us in this process. I have described some of these in *A Guide to Liberating Your Soul*. The bad news is that whichever way you tackle it, you are bound to encounter some emotional pain. The pain arises from the need to bring to the surface and let go of your deepest fears. The length of time it takes depends on the depth and extent of your fears.

Through working with the seven levels of leadership consciousness, I have come to recognize that there are different stages to leadership development. Stage 1 involves personal transformation. It supports the individual in releasing fears and becoming authentic. It is designed to take people from the lower three levels of consciousness to the level of facilitator leadership (level 4). Stage 2 builds emotional intelligence. It supports the individual in moving from the level of the facilitator (level 4) to the level of the collaborator (level 5). Stage 3 helps the individual become a builder of partnerships and strategic alliances. It supports the individual in moving from the level of collaborator (level 5) to the levels of servant/partner and wisdom/visionary (levels 6 and 7).

Each of the three stages of leadership development brings about a shift in personal awareness that leads to a higher state of consciousness. As individuals move from one level to the next, they expand their sense of identity by increasing their sense of connectedness to the world. During stage 1 training—personal transformation—they connect with their deepest self and attempt to become one with their soul. During stage 2 training—emotional intelligence—they learn to connect with their colleagues so that they can create a cohesive organizational culture. During stage 3 training they learn the importance of connecting with customers, suppliers, the local community, and society at large. Each of these stages is described in more detail next.

Stage 1: Becoming a Facilitator

Maslow described the work of transformation—moving from the consciousness of a manager to the consciousness of a facilitator—as self-actualization. It is about becoming an authentic individual, free from fear. Until individuals have learned to master their fears, understand their motivations, and are clear about their mission, they are unable to make decisions that fully support the good of the whole. Where there is fear, there is always self-interest. For this reason, the first stage of leadership training should focus on finding physical, emotional, mental, and spiritual balance and aligning one's personal mission, vision, and values with those of the organization. The underlying themes are self-knowledge and understanding the impact and limitations of fear. Leaders at this level need to know how to build a Balanced Needs Scorecard and how to create personal and organizational mission, vision, and values statements.

Stage 2: Becoming a Collaborator

The second stage of leadership development focuses on the development of an individual's emotional intelligence—building the communication skills that empower others and create organizational cohesion. To become an effective leader an individual should know how to create a sense of trust, openness, and empathy with others; build collaboration and team spirit; and give and receive effective feedback. They need to help others move beyond their limiting beliefs, access their creativity and intuition, and see problems as opportunities for growth. In addition to equipping an individual with these behavior-based communication skills, the stage 2 training should develop the leader's own intuition and creativity. Leaders at this level need to learn how to build a values-driven visionary organization and the principles of organizational evolution and renewal.

Stage 3: Becoming a Servant/Partner or Wisdom/Visionary

The third stage of leadership development focuses on raising individuals' awareness of their role, and their organization's role, in creating a sustainable future for humanity and the planet and the importance of partnering and strategic alliances to achieving long-lasting success. Participants learn what others are doing to combat the global crises that are threatening the social and environmental sustainability of life on the planet. They also learn, through case studies, how to form mutually supportive alliances and partnerships with customers, suppliers, and the local community. In addition to equipping the individual with information and knowledge on breaking down barriers, the stage 3 program teaches leaders how to deepen and strengthen their personal growth.

LEADERSHIP ASSESSMENT

It is important to assess what level of leadership development program is appropriate for a particular individual. The Leadership Values Assessment Instrument described in Chapter 5 can be used for this purpose. The instrument is very straightforward. Individuals complete self-assessments indicating what they believe are the values/behaviors that best describe their operational style. At the same time, ten or twelve colleagues assess the individual's operational style using the same values template. They also briefly describe the individual's strengths and weaknesses, and any other personal feedback they feel might be useful. The colleagues chosen should include superiors, peers, and subordinates. The results are aggregated so that the individual receives a collective assessment of his or her colleagues' feedback. A comparison of the individual's self-assessment with the results of the colleagues' assessment provides a rich data set that highlights the qualities of leadership that the individual embodies and those that need to be developed. The values assessment report highlights which of the three levels of leadership development would be most appropriate in supporting the individual in his or her leadership development.

The Leadership Assessment Instrument is particularly useful in building a cohesive management team. Each member of the team completes a self-assessment and a feedback assessment for other members of the team. The results of the feedback are aggregated and compared with the self-assessment. The individual members of the team share the results of the main findings of their personal reports with the other members of the team and seek their support in helping them to grow and develop as leaders. This level of sharing builds trust and mutually supportive relationships.

CASE STUDIES: LEADERSHIP ASSESSMENT

The following three case studies demonstrate the use of the Leadership Assessment Instrument. Terry, Pat, and Jack are part of a ten-member management team. Every member of the team has provided feedback for them. The results of the self-assessment are presented in the left-hand column and the results of the feedback from their nine colleagues are presented in the right-hand column. Each value is classified as positive or limiting depending on whether it supports or impedes the building of a cohesive organizational culture. The number of colleagues indicating that the individual displayed a particular value/behavior is shown in the column on the right. Only the top ten values/behaviors are shown. The center column indicates where there is a match between the individual's self-assessment and the colleagues' assessment.

Case Study: Terry

Five matches between Terry's assessment of his operating values/behaviors and his colleagues assessments indicate that Terry's

Self-Assessment

Vision
Ethics
Justice
Customer Collaboration
Mentoring
Balance Home/Work
Being the Best (L)
Competitive (L)
Extreme Loyalty (L)
Profit

PTOS (P) = 1-1-3-2
PTOS (L) = 0-3-0-0
PL = 7-3

Colleague's Assessment

Vision
Ethics
Customer Collaboration
Strategic Alliances
Honesty
Integrity
Balance Home/Work
Innovation
Being the Best (L)
Results Orientation

CTS = 54-19-27
PTOS (P) = 4-0-4-1
PTOS (L) = 0-1-0-0
PL = 9-1

Level	Self-Assessment	Match	Colleagues' Assessment
	Value, (Positive or Limiting)		Value, # of Votes, (Positive or Limiting)
7	Vision (P) Ethics (P) Justice (P)	↔ ↔	Vision 9 (P) Ethics 4 (P)
6	Customer Collaboration (P) Mentoring (P)	↔	Customer Collaboration 4 (P) Strategic Alliances 5 (P)
5			Honesty 4 (P) Integrity 3 (P)
4	Balance [Home and Work] (P)	↔	Balance [Home and Work] 3 (P) Innovation 4 (P)
3	Being the Best (L) Competitive (L)	↔	Being the Best 4 (L) Results Orientation 3 (P)
2	Extreme Loyalty (L)		
1	Profit (P)		

Colleagues' Assessment of Strengths
1. Clarity, intelligence, and knowledge.
2. Vision.

Colleagues' Assessment of Weaknesses
1. Poor communication with colleagues.
2. Lack of team-building skills.

Suggestions from Colleagues
1. Listen and communicate more with colleagues and less with the boss. Less personal ambition.

Figure 10–1
Terry: Leadership Values Assessment

perception of himself is similar to his colleagues' perception. This is generally a sign of authenticity and self-knowledge. Terry and his colleagues agree that he is well balanced. He also displays strong customer collaboration skills (level 6) and is concerned about vision and ethics (level 7). The areas of leadership that Terry needs to work on most are teamwork (level 4) and creating a sense of community (level 5). His colleagues would like him to communicate more and listen to their needs. They want him to be more of a team player and focus less on "being the best." Terry subconsciously knows that he is not good at building internal cohesion because he did not report any level 5 values in his self-assessment. In addition, he freely admitted that he is competitive, wants to be the best, and is extremely loyal. His loyalty is to the boss, not to the team.

Terry's CTS index, which measures the proportion of values in the upper three levels of consciousness (common good), the middle level (transformation), and the lower three levels (self-interest), is 54–19–27. Terry's CTS index is good. It could be improved by a stronger focus at the level of Transformation. Terry's chart shows that he has level 6 and 7 leadership qualities (ethics, vision, justice, customer collaboration, and strategic alliances) and level 5 and 4 personal qualities (honesty, integrity, innovation, and balance) but that he is short on level 5 and 4 community and team-building values.

Terry's colleague's assessment of his PTOS (P) index, which measures the number of personal, team, organizational, and societal values in his top ten values, is 4–0–4–1. They see him as having four personal values, four organizational values, and one societal value. They also see him as having one limiting team value—being the best. Terry gives himself a PTOS (P) index of 1–1–3–2 and a PTOS (L) index of 0–3–0–0. Of the four team values he ascribes to himself, three are potentially limiting.

Terry needs to work on releasing the fears that make him strongly competitive and wanting to outshine other team members. The associated behaviors are interfering with his ability to be a team player. At the same time, he needs to build his emotional intelligence skills so that he can relate to other management team members in a more positive way. Terry should be considering stage 1 and 2 leadership development programs to supplement his strong level 6 and 7 leadership skills.

Case Study: Pat

Like Terry, Pat has five matching values. Her perception of herself is very similar to her colleagues' perception. She shows up at work as an authentic individual. She has a very strong level 5 leadership style. More than 40 percent of her values are at the collaborator level of consciousness. Pat is also perceived as having good team-building skills (level 4). Her colleagues perceive her as giving strong emphasis to customer satisfaction and collaboration. She is not seen to be strong in strategic alliances (level 6), nor has she very many level 7 values. Her colleagues feel that Pat can be overly sensitive at times and they want her to be bolder in decision making. One other area of concern for Pat is the lack of values at level 1. She needs to become more focused on how her work relates to the bottom line.

Pat's CTS index is 60–16–24. This is a very strong index. A few more values at the level of transformation and few less at the levels of self-interest would make it even stronger. The score of 16 at the level of transformation may relate to the sensitivity that Pat exhibits to her team members' comments. The sensitivity she exhibits is related to her unresolved fears.

Pat's colleagues' assessment of her PTOS (P) index (3–3–4–0) is very close to her own assessment of (4–3–3–0). This is a well-balanced index with all positive values. The index could be improved slightly by reducing the number of organizational values and increasing the number of societal values.

Pat is very clearly a strong asset to the organization. She could improve her performance through stage 3 leadership development—strategic alliances and awareness raising to the role of her organization in the local community and society. Her sensitivity to her team members' comments suggests that she might also benefit from stage 1 leadership development. She needs to resolve her fears around feeling threatened by her colleagues' remarks.

Self-Assessment

Creativity
Excellence
Integrity
Process Orientation
Diversity
Teamwork
Empowerment
Customer Satisfaction
Respect
Results Orientation

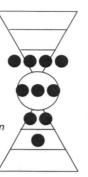

PTOS = 4-3-3-0
PL = 10-0

Colleague's Assessment

Customer Collaboration
Cooperation
Trust
Integrity
Honesty
Sense of Mission
Teamwork
Customer Satisfaction
Respect
Results Orientation

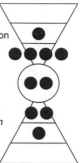

CTS = 60-16-24
PTOS = 3-4-4-0
PL = 10-0

Level	*Self-Assessment*	*Match*	*Colleagues' Assessment*
	Value, (Positive or Limiting)		Value, # of Votes, (Positive or Limiting)
7			
6			Customer Collaboration 6 (P)
5	Creativity (P) Excellence (P) Integrity (P) Process Orientation (P)	↔	Cooperation 8 (P) Trust 5 (P) Integrity 4 (P) Honesty 4(P)
4	Diversity (P) Teamwork (P) Empowerment (P)	↔	Sense of Mission 4 (P) Teamwork 3 (P)
3	Customer Satisfaction (P) Respect (P) Results Orientation (P)	↔ ↔ ↔	Customer Satisfaction 7 (P) Respect 6 (P) Results Orientation 4 (P)
2			
1			

Colleagues' Assessment of Strengths
1. Approachable, open, honest.
2. Smart, balanced, team player.

Colleagues' Assessment of Weaknesses
1. Can be overly sensitive sometimes.

Suggestions from Colleagues
1. Stop delaying decisions. Act more quickly.

Figure 10–2
Pat: Leadership Values Assessment

Self-Assessment

Long-Term Perspective
Customer Collaboration
Environmental Stewardship
Generosity
Creativity
Honesty
Humor/Fun
Balance Home/Work
Learning
Customer Satisfaction

PTOS = 7-0-2-1
PL = 10-0

Colleague's Assessment

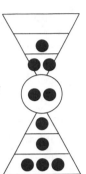

Community Work
Process Orientation
Commitment
Balance Home/Work
Knowledge
Productivity
Manipulation (L)
Territory (L)
Control (L)
Profit

CTS = 34-18-48
PTOS (P) = 3-0-3-1
PTOS (L) = 0-3-0-0
PL = 7-3

Level	*Self-Assessment*	*Match*	*Colleagues' Assessment*
	Value, (Positive or Limiting)		Value, # of Votes, (Positive or Limiting)
7	Long-term Perspective (P)		
6	Customer Collaboration (P)		Community Work 5 (P)
5	Social & Environmental Awareness (P) Generosity (P) Creativity (P) Honesty (P) Humor/Fun (P)		Process Orientation 6 (P) Commitment 4 (P)
4	Balance [Home and Work] (P) Learning (P)	↔	Balance [Home and Work] 5 (P) Knowledge 4 (P)
3	Customer Satisfaction (P)		Productivity 4 (P)
2			Manipulation 4 (L)
1			Territory 7 (L) Control 5 (L) Profit 4 (P)

Colleagues' Assessment of Strengths
1. Specialized knowledge and intelligence.

Colleagues' Assessment of Weaknesses
1. Lack of teamwork.

2. Little openness and collaboration.

Suggestions from Colleagues
1. Stop competing with your colleagues and understand it is one company.
2. Trust your people and delegate more.

Figure 10–3
Jack: Leadership Values Assessment

Case Study: Jack

Jack's perception of himself is quite different from that of his colleagues. The only agreement between Jack and his colleagues is that he has a good balance between his home and his work life. Jack's colleagues see him as being territorial, manipulative, and controlling. Jack does not recognize these behaviors in himself. He sees himself as honest, generous, creative, and fun loving. Jack is committed to his work (level 5) and is technically very sound (level 4). He is productive (level 3) and focused on making a profit (level 1). Jack is also concerned about his local community (level 6). Although Jack has some good qualities and is technically strong, his fears about trust and control cause him to be disruptive to the operation of the management team and the well-being of the company.

Jack's CTS index of 34–18–48 reflects his strong orientation toward self-interest rather than the common good. He is also relatively weak at the level of Transformation. His colleagues give him a PTOS (P) of 3–0–3–1 and a PTOS (L) of 0–3–0–0. They assign him three limiting team values. Jack gives himself a PTOS (P) of 7–0–2–1, confirming his lack of team values.

Jack's immediate need in terms of leadership development is personal transformation. If he is going to survive in the organization, he needs to release his fears about control. He must learn to trust others and become more collaborative.

Terry and Pat are clearly leadership material. Both are very authentic and have the majority of their values in the upper levels of consciousness. Terry has strong level 6 and 7 leadership styles but is less confident at levels 4 and 5. Pat, on the other hand, has a very strong level 5 leadership style. She also shows level 3 and 4 leadership skills. She is less strong at levels 6 and 7. Unlike Terry and Pat, Jack has a lot of work to do on himself if he is to become a leader. Jack will not progress unless he is able to release the fear-based beliefs that are causing him to be controlling, manipulative, and protective about his territory.

THE IMPORTANCE OF SELF-ACTUALIZATION

The preceding examples illustrate the importance of stage 1 leadership development (personal transformation). Even though Terry and Pat had high-level leadership skills, they still had fear-based issues that were affecting their work. Jack also needed stage 1 leadership development. Overcoming our personal fears and learning to empower others are fundamental skills that we all need to practice if we are to become visionary leaders. Almost everyone suffers from unresolved fear issues. At level 4 consciousness—transformation—we learn to shift from ego-centered consciousness to soul-centered consciousness. Even though we may have resolved the major fears in our lives and have developed some of the attributes of levels 5, 6, and 7 consciousness, there will always be some fears that remain unresolved. This is simply part of being human. Unresolved fears, about self-esteem, relationships, and survival, can very easily jeopardize the success of an organization. Therefore it is extremely important for those who are in leadership positions to learn to release these fears.

In *Driving Fear out of the Workplace*[2], Ryan and Oestreich catalog the impact of fear on 260 managers and employees from 22 organizations around the United States. They conclude that when people know in their bones that they are free to tell the truth about workplace problems or come forward with risky ideas for improvement without repercussions, quality and productivity flourish. The key issue about fear is their relationship with the boss. When employees do not have a manager they can trust, they become frustrated and work performance drops. The quality of the relationship employees have with their direct superior is a key determinant of the level of fear they experience at work. At least 70 percent of the 260 people that Ryan and Oestreich interviewed said they had hesitated to speak up because they feared some type of repercussion.[3] The authors estimate that the greatest percentage of intimidating behaviors is committed unconsciously by managers who have no idea how their behavior is affecting others.

Based on the responses of the interviewees, Ryan and Oestreich report the following impacts of fear. Twenty-nine percent of respondents noted negative feelings about the organization. One respondent noted that his organization had "Changed its relationship to its employees. Loyalty, trust and the family sense are gone. It's them and us—they would lay you off tomorrow if it fit a corporate interest. This certainly has reduced loyalty in return. I wouldn't recommend this organization to a friend." Twenty-seven percent of respondents noted a negative impact on quality or productivity. Nineteen percent noted negative feelings about themselves. Another 12 percent felt negative emotions.[4] When people feel afraid, they withdraw their allegiance to the organization and the boss. They "down tools" on their creativity and going the extra mile, because they are unwilling to take risks. You have to take risks to do good work. As fear accumulates in an organization, the commitment, motivation, confidence, and imagination of individuals diminish.

ETHICS, VALUES, AND BEHAVIORS

It would be useful at this point to show how ethics, values, and behaviors are linked. Ethics are value-based principles that we use to drive group decision making. They dictate how societies, communities, or organizations relate to one another, to individuals, and to their environment. They are often expressed as codes of conduct or guiding principles. When a group of individuals with a common interest develop a set of values regarding how they will operate, their values become codified as ethical principles. Thus, we find that many professions operate from a common set of ethical principles.

Whereas ethics operate at the macro level, values operate at the micro level. Values are personal. They dictate how individuals relate to one another and the environment and the planet. They operate at the level of interactions between individuals within a society, a community, or an organization. When a group of people agree to abide by a common set of values, they build a sense of community. The acting out of these values within the group creates a sense of trust. When the agreed values are not acted out, trust breaks down and the sense of community disappears.

Although we can talk and write about our ethics and values, they become tangible only when they are expressed as behaviors. The way to determine individuals' values is by studying their behaviors. It is not what I say but what I do that informs you of my values. Integrity occurs when there is alignment between an individual's stated values and behaviors. People with unresolved fears compromise their integrity. Without integrity there can be no trust.

Personal values express the relationship content of our deeply held beliefs. They originate from one of two sources— love* or fear. A distinguishing characteristic of beliefs based on fear is that they cause us to behave *reactively*. A certain event or situation will trigger a subconscious fear that causes us to protect ourselves or what we covet. Our reaction always serves our perceived self-interest. For example, let's say I am a very ambitious person and my company hires a bright new employee that I see as a possible competitor for a senior management position that I had been hoping to get. One day this person approaches me for some important information that could help him with his work. I respond by saying I am willing to help, but in fact I find excuse after excuse to delay our meeting. My behavior is determined by my fear. It is not immediately obvious to an observer why I am acting this way. To get to the real reason for my behavior, we have to delve into four levels of explanation.

The first level of explanation might be that I am not able to meet with this person because I have other urgent matters to attend to. The second level of explanation might be that I am an uncooperative person. The third level of explanation gets closer to the truth. I am being uncooperative because this person is a competitor for the job that I covet. At the next level of explanation we find the truth. The fourth level of explanation is that I have a problem with self-esteem. I have a fear-based belief that says that I am

---

* I use the term love in its broadest context to include connectedness, benevolence, enthusiasm, and community.

not respected. I believe that if I get the job, I will become more respected because I will increase my status. Therefore, my uncooperative stance is really about my fear of not being respected.

The major difference between beliefs based on fear and beliefs based on love is that the latter allow us to choose consciously our response to a particular situation. Beliefs based on fear always trigger an emotional response that is designed to serve our personal self-interest. In such situations, we operate with *react*-ability rather than *response*-ability. Fear always restricts our domain of action. Love, on the other hand, expands our options. When our values are based on love, we can choose how we wish to respond.

A significant proportion of the personal values we exhibit in the lower three levels of human consciousness are motivated by fear. All the personal values we exhibit in the upper three levels of consciousness are motivated by love. Level 4 is the transition point where an individual or an organization shifts from a belief system based primarily on fear to a belief system based primarily on love. As an individual makes this transition, he or she retains the positive values from the lower levels of consciousness but gives up the negative values. We are able to grow into the higher levels of consciousness when we overcome our fears and learn to embrace truth and love.[5] Maslow points out that healthy growth is a never-ending series of choices between safety (fear) and growth (love).

SOME BASIC PRINCIPLES FOR LEADERSHIP DEVELOPMENT PROGRAMS

For organizations to get the most out of their leadership training budgets, it is important to abide by the following principles.

Standardize the Program

A standardized leadership program, either internal or external, helps to develop common concepts and a common language that become ingrained in the organizational culture. A sense of camaraderie builds around those who have taken the same training courses. When the training is standardized, alumni are more able to support one another in implementing what they have learned.

Leaders and Managers Should Experience the Same Training

Millions of dollars are wasted every year by organizations that send their managers on leadership and personal awareness training but fail to send the president or vice presidents. The managers return to the organization keen to implement their newfound skills and understanding but quickly become disenchanted when their new behaviors are not mirrored by their bosses. In such cases the training alienates the managers from the company rather than strengthening their loyalties. They become more aware of the lack of alignment between their personal values and the organization's values. Ideally, the leaders and top managers should be the first ones to experience the leadership training. The training should then cascade down through the organization.

The Training Should Support the Culture

The training should be tailored to support the organizational culture. This particularly applies to the values, mission, and vision and Balanced Needs Scorecard training. All employees need to know how their personal mission, vision, and values link to the organization's mission, vision, and values. They also need to feel a sense of ownership and responsibility for the well-being of the company. Open-book management based on a Balanced Needs Scorecard allows them to be kept fully informed and knowledgeable about the organization's performance and progress.

The Culture Should Support the Training

In a similar vein, the incentives in the human resource processes should be in alignment with the leadership training. When employees learn in training that certain values are important to the organization, it is important that they see those who are being promoted or hired as having the values that the organization says it wants to develop. Then and only then will they regard the training as relevant to their advancement.

The importance of leadership assessment and identifying the appropriate level of leadership training cannot be overemphasized. Every individual comes to the workplace with different issues that need to be resolved. Many CEOs and senior executives make the mistake of believing that because they have made it to the top they don't need leadership training. This is a false assumption. Leaders owe it to their colleagues and stockholders to be continually concerned about their self-development They need to pay particular attention to their unresolved fears. The values and behaviors that leaders bring to the workplace can have a significant impact, both positive and negative, on the performance of the organization as a whole.

Notes

1. Richard Barrett, *A Guide to Liberating Your Soul* (Alexandria: Fulfilling Books, 1995).

2. Kathleen D. Ryan and Daniel K. Oestreich, *Driving Fear out of the Workplace: How to Overcome the Invisible Barriers to Quality, Productivity, and Innovation* (San Francisco: Jossey-Bass, 1991).

3. Ibid., p. 6.

4. Ibid., p. 57.

5. Abraham Maslow, *Toward a Psychology of Being* (New York: Van Nostrand Reinhold, 1982).

11

Building a Visionary Organization

The next wave of enduring great companies will be built not by technical or product visionaries but by social visionaries—those who see their company and how it operates as their ultimate creation and who invent entirely new ways of organizing human effort and creativity.

—JIM COLLINS

The driving thrust of our company, from the day it was founded, was renewal. So we've never had to discover the need for change.

—ROBERT W. GALVIN, CHAIRMAN OF THE BOARD, MOTOROLA

Over the years we developed not only a different strategy, but also a different strategy planning process. Basically we just don't do it. In an industry where a two week plan is likely to become obsolete . . . it is a meaningless exercise.

—HERB KELLEHER, CEO, SOUTHWEST AIRLINES

The assumptions that have driven all of Procter & Gamble's organization designs are that (1) people want to be responsible, (2) they are capable of directing themselves, (3) they can work collaboratively, in alignment . . . with common goals; and (4) the majority of improvements or innovations ultimately come from individuals whose personal interests are congruent with those of the organization.

—MANAGER AT PROCTER & GAMBLE

THE CHARACTERISTICS OF LONG-LASTING SUCCESSFUL ORGANIZATIONS

My purpose in this chapter is to draw together the models and tools described in earlier chapters and show how they form a comprehensive framework for building a visionary organization. I define a visionary organization as a long-living, successful organization that cares about its employees, its customers, the local community, the environment, and society at large. Visionary organizations take social responsibility very seriously. They display six important characteristics:

1. They have strong, positive, values-driven cultures.
2. They make a lasting commitment to learning and self-renewal.
3. They are continually adapting themselves based on feedback from internal and external environments.
4. They make strategic alliances with internal and external partners, customers, and suppliers.
5. They are willing to take risks and experiment.
6. They have a balanced values-based approach to measuring performance that includes such factors as
   - Corporate survival (financial results)
   - Corporate fitness (efficiency, productivity, and quality)
   - Collaboration with suppliers and customers
   - Continuous learning and self-development (Corporate Evolution)
   - Organizational cohesion and employee fulfillment (Corporate Culture)
   - Corporate contribution to the local community and society

A Values-Driven Culture

A strong positive culture is one in which values are shared. Everyone is working toward creating the same vision of the future and people are able to find personal fulfillment at work by satisfying their physical, emotional, mental, and spiritual needs.

Visionary companies work very hard at building and maintaining such a culture. They constantly assess how well they are doing in living their values.

Visionary organizations are not only aware of their values, they consciously use them to guide decision making and to build a cohesive corporate culture. Visionary organizations primarily operate from the higher levels of the Seven Levels of Corporate Consciousness and have values that support the good of the whole. They find a dynamic balance between the organization's needs for survival and growth; the employees' needs for personal fulfillment; the local community's and society's needs for economic, social, and environmental sustainability; and stockholders' needs for financial success.

Learning and Self-Renewal

Continuous self-renewal is possible only when an organization is willing to question its basic assumptions and motivations, to make a commitment to learning, and to remain open to opportunities for self-development. Most established companies fail because they develop rigid beliefs. They become complacent and arrogant in their success. They believe they know all the answers. This type of thinking is the anathema of self-renewal. When an organization can no longer maintain its viability, it must either transform or die. In such situations, change is not enough. A radical shift in beliefs and values is required that leads to a new way of being. Change in the form of reengineering can reduce costs and improve efficiency, but it cannot build a new culture.

Visionary companies, like visionary individuals, are never satisfied with their achievements. They continually search for ways to improve their products and services. They are always willing to question their guiding assumptions and stay in touch with their motivations. If their guiding assumptions or motivations change, they are ready to reinvent themselves. The way they evaluate their assumptions and motivations is through learning— both externally and internally. They research their markets and the trends that affect their business. They inquire into the internal workings of the organization and the needs of their employees. They are willing to explore the psyche of the organization and are always listening and enquiring. Visionary companies do not compete with other companies, they compete against themselves.

Adaptation Based on Feedback

During times of rapid change, the organizations that survive and are successful are those that are able to adapt to their environments. This is a principle of evolution. At this time in history we are experiencing a rapid change in technology and a rapid change in values. The only way that companies will stay alive is to embrace evolution. Evolution most easily occurs in systems that are internally cohesive (strong core culture), have multiple channels of open communication (boundaryless), are dedicated to learning, and have a profound commitment to self-development.

Evolution is a continual state of change and transformation. Transformation occurs when organizations and individuals embrace self-development and are willing to replace beliefs and assumptions that no longer work with a new way of being. When organizations continually question their assumptions and motivations, evolution can take place. Visionary organizations stay open to feedback from employees, customers, suppliers, and society at large. They are constantly adapting to their internal and external environments. A visionary organization continually adjusts its business strategy and culture to develop itself and support the common good.

Ilya Prigogine's Nobel Prize-winning "Theory of Dissipative Structures" offers a scientific model that explains the critical role of transformation in evolution. According to Prigogine, some forms of nature are open systems, continuously exchanging energy with their environment, whereas other forms are closed. A seed that becomes a plant and an organization that is successful over a long period of time are both examples of open systems. A rock is an example of a closed system. Open systems have permeable boundaries that allow new energy to flow in and out freely. Closed systems, on the other hand, block the movement of energy. They cannot grow and evolve because they are unable or refuse to interact with outside influences. When systems regard themselves as separate rather than interdependent, they tend to stay the same while the outside world changes. Eventually, they lose touch with external reality and become stressed by trying to survive in a world that has left them behind. When the stress becomes intolerable, it precipitates into an existential crisis; the outcome of which is transformation or death.

Another essential difference between open and closed systems is the degree of internal cohesion. When organizations are heavily structured with strong hierarchical controls, internal boundaries prevent the flow of information and there is very little cohesion. When organizations are unstructured with a multitude of informal networks, the system is more complex. But it is also more intricately connected because there are fewer blockages to the flow of information. The Internet and e-mail support this type of exchange. In open systems, avenues for the exchange of information occur naturally. Information is able to flow freely because there are fewer boundaries and fiefdoms that block the information flow. General Electric's boundaryless organization is an example of an attempt to put this concept into practice.

Strategic Alliances

Visionary organizations create trusting relationships with their customers, suppliers, and the local community by forming long-term strategic alliances and partnerships. Such alliances help the organizations anticipate trends, streamline production, cut costs, and build goodwill. When customers and suppliers are invited to become part of the design team, the organization is able to integrate the concerns of the producer and the end user in a holistic systematic manner. This type of integration is especially helpful when the product being sold is used by the client to make products for its clients (for example, the machine tool industry). The closer an organization can get to integrating the concerns of the ultimate beneficiary (the customer's customer) into their design and production process, the more successful the product.

Strategic alliances with the local community not only build goodwill but also become a source of employee pride. When employees feel good about their organization, they are more loyal and willing to go the extra mile. Allowing employees to do volunteer work in the local community on company time gives employees an opportunity to find personal fulfillment. They feel that the organization is supporting them in being of service and making a difference. This is one of the highest forms of personal fulfillment.

Risk Taking and Experimentation

Visionary organizations know that to be successful they must experiment and take risks. They cannot rely totally on customer collaboration to define their product line. New technologies are creating opportunities for products and services that customers could never have envisaged. Risk taking and experimentation must become part of the culture. If new ideas are to be encouraged, fear must be banished. This will happen only if the culture is able to celebrate failure as well as success. Failures must be redefined as collective learning opportunities. In visionary organizations, everyone learns from everyone else's mistakes as well as their successes.

Balance

Visionary organizations measure their progress against a values-driven Balanced Needs Scorecard. This scorecard measures the inputs and outputs of their physical, emotional, mental, and spiritual well-being. Measurement is key. Whatever is measured tends to improve. Visionary organizations recognize that financial success is the result of setting and meeting targets that focus on such inputs as corporate fitness, customer and supplier collaboration, corporate evolution, corporate culture, and contribution to the local community and society. When an organization focuses on a balanced set of inputs and keeps a tight reign on costs, profits take care of themselves.

BUILDING AND MAINTAINING A VISIONARY ORGANIZATION

Based on the preceding findings, I have developed a three-phase process for building a visionary organization that is supported by the Corporate Transformation Models and Tools. A flow diagram of the process is shown in Figure 11–1.

Preparation

Step 1: Secure Leadership Commitment to Develop a Values-Driven Culture

Once a leader is convinced that cultural change is necessary, his or her first task is to develop a compelling case for action. If the organization is doing well, then the leader's approach should be that of a visionary setting out the next stage in the development of the organization. If the organization is doing badly, then the leader's approach should be one of taking corrective actions to bring about organizational renewal.

If the corrective actions involve reengineering, the approach taken should reflect the values that the new culture is trying to promote (participation, fairness, openness, and trust). Any other approach will simply undermine the establishment of the new culture. There must be total integrity between the espoused values and the organization's behaviors. In either case, visionary development or corrective action, the leader must gain the commitment of the leadership team.

If the organizational transformation is to be successful, all individuals in the leadership team must be willing to take a hard look at their own personal values and behaviors and make the adjustments that are necessary to embrace the new culture. Organizations don't transform. People do! Without this personal commitment, cultural change will not happen.

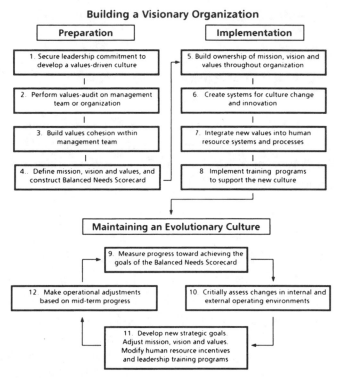

Figure 11-1
Building a Visionary Organization

Many employees, and particularly managers, may find the adjustment challenging. The switch from controller to coach, and from manager to mentor, demands a shift in consciousness that many find difficult. Those who are able to transform themselves will find a new sense of meaning in their work. Those who are unable to change will eventually leave.

Step 2. Perform Corporate Culture Assessment
Once the leadership team has committed to building a values-driven organization, the next step is to carry out a detailed assessment of the organization's existing culture. The Values Audit Instrument has been designed for this purpose. It identifies the organization's top ten values and distribution of consciousness. It also assesses the degree of alignment between personal values

and organizational values, between organizational values and ideal organizational values, and between the espoused culture and the actual culture. The major benefit of the values audit is that it makes the "soft stuff" hard. It allows an organization to establish a baseline and set identifiable goals and targets for monitoring cultural change.

The instrument is simple to administer and the results can be disaggregated vertically and horizontally. By including demographic data, values can be assessed by gender, length of service, age, or any other grouping factor that can readily be measured. Twelve months later, the same tool can be used to provide an assessment against the baseline of the progress that has been made toward achieving the new culture.

The values audit serves several purposes.

- It provides information on the strengths and weaknesses of the existing culture.
- It identifies the direction and priorities for change.
- It provides a justification for action.

Step 3: Build Values Cohesion within the Leadership Team

If transformation is to be successful, all members of the leadership team must commit to the culture change and be willing to tackle their own leadership issues. The cultural transformation must begin at the top and work its way through the organization. If the leadership team as a whole is not able to model the new values and behaviors, the next level of management will not buy into the change.

The Leadership Values Assessment Instrument has been designed to assist managers in identifying their leadership issues. Based on the results of the leadership assessment, each member of the leadership team should commit to a personal leadership training program and seek the support of the others to help them tackle their leadership issues. A mutually supportive and trusting environment must be created in the leadership team if it is to manage the cultural change successfully. Most leadership issues can be handled by one of the three types of leadership training. In some cases, personal mentoring or coaching may be required. Visionary leaders know that if they want their senior people to change, they must lead the way by tackling their own leadership issues openly and willingly.

Step 4: Review Mission, Vision, and Values and Construct Balanced Needs Scorecard

The last step in the preparatory phase is for the leadership team to define the direction and strategy of transformation; identify the criteria the organization will use to measure success; and set out the framework, process, and timetable for the implementation of the cultural transformation.

The direction of the transformation is defined by the mission, vision, and values. The "Four Why's" process provides a powerful framework for defining the organization's core business and how it will find internal and external fulfillment. The transformational strategy is defined by the organization's Balanced Needs Scorecard. The mission, vision, and values provide the framework within which the goals, objectives, and targets of the scorecard are defined. The objectives and targets will be the criteria the organization will use to measure success. The leadership team's task is to prepare a first draft of the mission, vision, and values and the Balanced Needs Scorecard. Feedback should be sought from employees during the implementation phase before the vision, mission, and values and Balanced Needs Scorecard are finalized.

An important part of the process of defining the organization's direction is for all members of the leadership team to identify and relate their own mission and vision to those of the organization. Everyone in the leadership team needs to know how they can support their colleagues in helping each other find personal fulfillment in their work. It is important that the leadership team does this exercise together so that they are fully aware of how their collective motivations interact. In small organizations and start-up companies, it is recommended that the process of defining the organization's direction begins with identifying the personal missions and visions of the founding members and staff.

These missions and visions are the fundamental driving forces of the organization. They need to be harnessed and fully integrated into the organization's mission and vision if the organization is to be successful.

The last steps in this initial phase are to (a) develop a framework, process, and timetable for the implementation phase of the new culture; (b) develop a compelling justification for change based on business projections and the values audit; and (c) establish a sense of urgency. At this point, the proposed transformation can be communicated to the employees and the implementation can begin.

Assessing the Organization's Readiness for Transformation
It is important to assess the readiness of an organization for cultural change before the implementation phase begins. Readiness depends on two factors: (a) the commitment of the leader and the leadership team to personal transformation and (b) a cultural predisposition to transformation within the organization. Organizational transformation will not occur if the leadership team is not able to walk the new talk and there is no organizational predisposition to the values and behaviors that promote internal cohesion—trust, integrity, openness, and transparency. It will be obvious from the results of the values audit and the leadership assessment of the leadership team whether the organization should proceed with implementation or should spend more time in working through issues that could block the transformation process.

Implementation

Step 5: Build Ownership of Vision, Mission, and Values and Balanced Needs Scorecard Throughout the Organization

For cultural transformation to be successful, everyone in the organization must own and live the new vision, mission, and values. Therefore it is important to let *all* employees know that their opinions are important and that they will be invited to participate. The engagement with employees begins by informing them of the leadership team's assessment of the situation and reasons for change (step 4). The draft vision, mission, and values statements should then be shared with employees and their ideas and comments sought. Only when this process is complete should the statements be finalized.

Although this makes a good start at establishing ownership, the discussion needs to be taken to a deeper level. This deeper level of employee involvement is achieved by establishing motivational connections between the organization's vision and mission and the mission of each work unit and every employee. If employees are to find personal fulfillment, they need to establish a connection between their own work motivations and the motivations of the company. Without this alignment, employees will not find personal fulfillment through their work.

A similar approach needs be taken with the Balanced Needs Scorecard. The goals, objectives, and targets will not be owned by the employees unless they are involved in the process of defining them. Whereas the leadership team is best placed to develop the overall strategy and translate it into specific goals, individual work units are in a much better position to define the objectives and targets. Allowing people who do the work to set their own objectives and stretch targets is always more productive than having them handed down from above. People become more emotionally committed to targets they set themselves than those that are set for them. The goals, objectives, and targets of the Balanced Needs Scorecard together with the monitored monthly or quarterly results should be communicated frequently to staff. The principles of open-book management should be used to communicate the organization's performance. The fundamental purpose of training employees to understand every aspect of the Balanced Needs Scorecard is to encourage them to think like owners.

Step 6: Create Systems to Oversee Culture and Innovation Development

An essential step in the implementation process is to create two cross-organizational committees (a) to oversee the implementation and maintenance of the new culture and (b) to institutionalize the search for innovative ideas. The purpose of the culture committee is to promote employee fulfillment and create a climate of creativity in which the minds of *all* employees can be brought to bear on the critical issues facing the organization. The purpose of the innovation committee is to foster innovation by creating mechanisms whereby new ideas are translated into both process and product improvements.

Culture Committee
The first step in institutionalizing the search for innovative ideas should be to establish a culture of employee participation and transparency. The old paradigm of management as the mind and the workers as the body needs to be laid to rest. The following comment of a worker at a Fortune 500 company is particularly relevant: "For twenty years I gave you the work of my hands. If you had asked you could have had my mind also." In the twenty-first century every ounce of intellectual and emotional intelligence that the organization can muster will be necessary for success. Employees need to know what is going on in the company and that their ideas are encouraged and valued before they will share their creativity. Equally important is the need to create a climate of trust in which people are not afraid to speak up. The Culture Committee should include a broad spectrum of individuals representing the full diversity of the organization.

Increasingly, organizations are creating senior management positions that focus on corporate culture. Examples of job titles include Vice President for Corporate Culture and Director of Employee Fulfillment. Their primary role is to oversee the implementation, development, and maintenance of the corporate culture. In a visionary company this involves monitoring the corporate culture on a regular basis to make sure the espoused values are being lived, developing leadership training programs that focus on building internal cohesion and empowering employees, seeking to assist employees in finding personal fulfillment through their work, making sure human resource systems and processes support the corporate culture, selecting new employees whose values are aligned to the corporate culture, and making the organization a fun place to work.

Innovation Committee

The work of the Innovation Committee is to generate ideas that could lead to process and product improvements. The committee should create mechanisms for encouraging and evaluating employee's ideas. It should also set up mechanisms whereby customers and suppliers can contribute ideas. The challenge the Innovation Committee faces is to provide a pipeline of product innovations that keeps the organization ahead of its competitors and process innovations that lead to reductions in cost or improvements in quality.

Step 7: Integrate the Espoused Values into Human Resource Systems and Processes

The greatest leverage an organization has for successfully implementing and maintaining a long-term cultural shift is to introduce the espoused values and behaviors into the human resource evaluation processes. The espoused values must be totally reflected in the criteria that are used for promotion or demotion and for hiring and firing staff. Only individuals who display the espoused values and behaviors should be promoted or hired. In the long-term, cultural compatibility is more important to visionary organizations than hiring or promoting excellent technical people who cannot build trust, empower others, or create internal cohesion.

The Leadership Values Assessment Instrument described in Chapter 5 can be used to assess an employee's progress in integrating the new values into his or her organizational behavior patterns. The instrument provides valuable feedback for the employee on their authenticity, the types of values they exhibit, and areas they need to work on to become more aligned with the espoused culture.

The Employee Entry Assessment Instrument allows an employer to assess how well an applicant's organizational values align with the espoused corporate culture. The instrument identifies the degree of alignment of the candidate's organizational values with the values of the organization's "ideal employees," and the degree of alignment of the candidate's organizational values with the espoused culture of the organization as expressed in the vision, mission, and values statements.

Step 8: Implement Training Programs to Support the New Culture

Three types of training are needed to support the new culture— training that supports employees in finding meaning through their work by aligning their personal work mission with the organization's vision, mission, and values (extension of step 5); training that helps employees understand how the tasks they perform make a difference to the success of the organization as measured through the Balanced Needs Scorecard goals, objectives, and targets (extension of step 5); and training that supports managers in becoming leaders (extension of step 3 involving managers throughout the whole company).

Alignment with the Organization's Mission and Vision

If an organization wants to harness the highest levels of productivity and creativity of its employees, it must find ways to align the personal motivations of each employee with work that supports the vision and mission of the organization. In visionary organizations managers are fully attuned to the importance of creating opportunities for all employees to be involved in work that allows them to express their sense of mission or inner potential. If employees are unaware of their inner potential, they need to be encouraged to determine how they find meaning in their lives.

Alignment with Balanced Needs Scorecard

Employees need to know precisely on a day-to-day basis how the tasks they perform contribute to the overall success of the company (Balanced Needs Scorecard). When they understand this link, they are able to see how they can improve the performance of the organization. When employees do not know how their work affects the success of the organization (the goals of the Balanced Needs Scorecard), they are unable to measure their performance or see how their work is making a difference. People who work together in teams need to be able to share their personal motivations so that they can support each other in finding personal fulfillment.

Leadership Development

Leadership training should focus on personal transformation (releasing fears), building emotional intelligence, and learning to think globally. Maintaining a values-driven organizational culture requires a shift in emphasis from managership to leadership and from intellectual intelligence to emotional intelligence. It requires people who are authentic, identify with the common good, and are balanced in their approach to life. In short, it requires self-actualized individuals who operate primarily from the higher levels of consciousness. There is no room for selfishness in a values-driven organization.

Leadership training should support managers in learning how to find meaning; make a difference; and be of service by empowering employees, building internal cohesion, developing strategic alliances, and supporting the common good. The biggest resistance to changing to a values-driven culture will come from managers whose personal values are strongly founded in the lower levels of consciousness. To shift to the new culture, they will need to face up to the fears they hold about their survival, status, and self-esteem.

Maintenance

The focus of steps 1 through 8 is on the structural aspects of building a new culture and developing a values-based method of defining success. The focus of steps 9 through 12 is on measuring performance and strategic renewal. Once the training programs described in step 8 have been implemented, the process of creating a visionary organization moves into an evolutionary spiral of continuous renewal. This is achieved through mechanisms that provide regular feedback about (a) progress in meeting the targets of the Balanced Needs Scorecard and (b) the organization's internal and external environment. As we have discussed, evolution is a state of continual transformation and change. It involves the constant review and reflection about beliefs, values, and behaviors based on learning gained from measurement of performance and feedback from internal and external environments. The last four steps in building a visionary organization outline the process of self-renewal.

Step 9: Measure Progress Toward Achieving the Goals and Objectives of the Balanced Needs Scorecard

The mechanism that visionary organizations use for measuring performance and implementing strategic renewal is some form of Balanced Needs Scorecard. It should give the organization a way of measuring its physical, emotional, mental, and spiritual well-being.

Step 10: Critically Assess Changes in Internal and External Operating Environments

The mechanism that visionary organizations use for determining the direction of strategic renewal is feedback from the organization's internal and external environments. As part of the annual review of organizational performance, the Culture Committee should develop a critical assessment of the internal culture (values audit). The culture report should contain information on the actual values compared with the espoused values, the distribution of consciousness, the types of values, and the strength of the culture.

Simultaneously, the Innovation Committee needs to develop a critical assessment of the external operating environment. The report should not be limited to the field of operation of the organization. It should cover major trends in societal values, population dynamics, education, politics, environment, and technology. This type of information, customized for particular sectors, is readily available from professional trend watchers. Understanding and interpreting the impact of these trends on the mission and vision of the organization and the values that support employee fulfillment, customer satisfaction, and societal goodwill are essential for strategic renewal. In larger organizations this information is used to carry out scenario-based planning—examining possible futures and the impact they may have on services and products.

The result of the critical assessment of internal and external operating environments should manifest as changes in the mission, vision, or values of the organization and/or changes in the goals that drive the six categories of the Balanced Needs Scorecard. Whereas it is usual to make changes to the Balanced Needs Scorecard every year, it is less usual to update the vision, mission, and values every year. It is important, however, to have a mechanism whereby the vision, mission, and values can be reviewed regularly in case changes are necessary.

Step 11: Review/Adjust Balanced Needs Scorecard and Vision, Mission, and Values

Based on the results of the critical assessments of the internal and external operating environments and progress in attaining the objectives of the Balanced Needs Scorecard, the management team adjusts the goals and objectives of the Balanced Needs Scorecard and, if necessary, fine tunes the vision, mission, and values. The management team's proposals are then communicated to the line managers and their staff, who review the changes and define targets for the following year. These are fed back to the management team, who finalize the adjustments and communicate them through meetings, training programs, and information bulletins to all staff.

Some companies solicit changes in their vision, mission, and values from staff on a regular basis. Johnson & Johnson for example invite all employees to put forward their suggestions for modifying the mission, vision and values statements every two years. Ralph S. Larsen, CEO of Johnson & Johnson, calls the credo statement the heart of their values system. He adds, "The only way to keep values alive is to continue to talk about them, to study them, to live them."[1]

Step 12: Make Operational Adjustments Based on Midterm Progress

A well-designed Balanced Needs Scorecard provides monthly and quarterly measures of performance in each category of the scorecard using lead and lag indicators. The constant monitoring of this information allows organizations to identify blockages to progress and to take rapid action. A formal mechanism for reviewing progress on *all* indicators is recommended every six months. In addition, some indicators will need to be monitored on a monthly or quarterly basis. Initially, during the first 12 to 24 months of a cultural transformation, a sample values audit should be undertaken every 6 months.

STRATEGIC PLANNING

The four-step process of maintaining an evolutionary culture by adjusting the Balanced Needs Scorecard and vision, mission, and values provides a comprehensive strategic planning process. The advantages of this system are that (a) it is responsive to short-term feedback, (b) it focuses on the total well-being of the organization, and (c) it is driven by the organization's motivations and values. In a world where technical, economic, and social change is accelerating exponentially, the value of long-term planning is questionable. Nor does it make much sense to think in terms of rigid organizational structures. They can easily become straightjackets that prevent the organization from making rapid responses to changing environments. Herb Kelleher, Chairman, President, and CEO of the extremely successful Southwest Airlines, has the following to say about strategic planning: "Over the years we developed a different strategy planning process. Basically, we just don't do it. In an industry where a two-week plan is likely to become obsolete, to spend days debating whether we're going to serve Trenton, New Jersey, in 2003 is a meaningless exercise. Rather than trying to predict what we'll do, we try to define who we are and what we want in terms of market niche, operational strategy and financial health. We reflect, observe, debate—and we don't use our calculators. Our strategic planning is an effort to establish flexible goals and guideposts, not detailed action steps."[2]

SMALL AND LARGE ORGANIZATIONS

The process of building a visionary organization is equally applicable to small (less than 50 people), medium (50 to 200), and large (200+) organizations. The principal difference is the amount of time needed. A significant cultural change can be implemented in small companies in a matter of six to eight months. In large companies it may take two years or longer. Factors that could increase the amount of time required to bring about transformation are the availability of budget and the degree of resistance to change. In well-established cultures that are focused in the lower levels of consciousness (self-interest), the resistance to change will come primarily from those who believe they have something to lose. Having strived to get to where they are by aligning themselves with the old culture, many of them will be upset by a change in the rules. They will have to change their behaviors to be effective in the new environment. This can be very threatening. Some managers will be unable to make the shift and will leave.

The critical factors in successful transformations are (a) the management team's commitment to modeling the new values and behaviors; (b) integrating the new values into the structural incentives of the human resource processes of the organization; (c) building psychological ownership by involving employees in defining the mission, vision, and values and the Balanced Needs Scorecard objectives and targets; (d) helping employees to think like owners; and (e) assigning responsibilities and developing structural mechanisms to support innovation, learning, and cultural renewal.

Notes

1. R. Levering and M. Moskowitz, *The 100 Best Companies to Work for in America* (New York: Currency Doubleday, 1994), p. 210.

2. H. Kelleher, "A Culture of Commitment," *Leader to Leader*, Spring 1997, pp. 20–24.

12

The New Theories of Business

As we move into the twenty-first century it is clear that the old paradigm of business is foundering. The theories of business that created the modern age are no longer serving companies and they are no longer serving society. The new theories that are emerging protect and sustain our environment; treat people and communities with respect; and serve the common good. We are entering into the era of compassionate capitalism. The new theories of business are founded around seven principles.

Principle 1: Who You Are and What You Stand for Are Just as Important as What You Sell.

It is no longer sufficient to deliver a great product or service, you must also live by rules that support the common good. There is a growing awareness all over the world that the greed and self-interest of business are at the core of so many of society's ills. The most successful companies in the twenty-first century will be those that are responsible members of the community and good global citizens. They will be seeking to align the company's values with society's values. The values that companies live by will play an increasingly important role in the public's purchasing decisions and the quality of employees that a company can attract.

Principle 2: Investment in Personal Fulfillment is Essential for High Performance.

As competition increases through the globalization of the economy, companies will increasingly recognize that their competitive advantage lies in tapping the deepest levels of their employees' productivity, creativity, and knowledge. To do this, they must invest in their cultural capital. They will need to focus on creating a corporate culture and working environment that brings personal fulfillment to everyone in the organization. This means caring for the physical, emotional, mental and spiritual needs of their employees. Work/life programs will not be sufficient. Companies will need to invite employee participation, provide work that gives their lives meaning and align employees' work with their mission. They will need to create a climate of trust and openness that encourages employees to become all they can become and bring their whole selves to work.

Principle 3. Relationships Are the Engines of Success.

Building a climate of trust and employee fulfillment requires emotional intelligence. The ability to empathize and empower people to become all they can become requires personal skills that are not taught in business schools. The companies of the future are staffing themselves with educated, self-actualized individuals who have plumbed the depths of self-knowledge, people who know how to relate to other human beings not from a position of self-interest but from a position of the good of the whole. In companies of the future, the values you express and how you relate to others will become the new pathways to promotion. Knowing how to create positive stakeholder relationships with employees, customers, suppliers, the local community, society, and stockholders are becoming the fundamental elements for long-term success.[1, 2]

Principle 4. Vision, Evolution and Transformation Drive Long-term Growth.

Forget change. Successful businesses of the future will be embracing transformation. Change is doing what we do now, but doing it more efficiently or productively. Transformation is about a new way of being. Transformation embraces the concept of change, but it adds something new. It questions basic operating assumptions. In so doing, it invites you to look at your work from a systems perspective. Transformation can happen only if leaders are willing to live in a state of openness and question their most cherished beliefs. Evolution occurs when organizations are able to live in a constant state of transformation. The companies that survive this unprecedented time of change will be those that embrace evolution. Vision gives direction to an organization's evolution. But the vision, like a business's operating assumptions, must be constantly examined.

Principle 5. Organizational Transformation Begins at the Top.

Organizations don't transform. People do. Corporate culture is fundamentally a function of the personality of the leadership. If you want to transform your company then you must first transform the belief systems, values, and behaviors of your top people. Millions of dollars are wasted each year sending middle managers on personal development courses. They taste and experience transformation. When they return, they find their newly acquired knowledge and skills are not appreciated by their superiors. The training serves only to frustrate and alienate managers from the company. If the management team is not able to model the values and behaviors that are conducive to creating a high performance twenty-first century organization then there will be no organizational transformation. No matter what your position in a company, if you want to transform your organization, you must start by transforming yourself. Leaders owe it to their colleagues and shareholders to be continually concerned about their personal development. Personal transformation training is becoming an essential aspect of professional growth.

Principle 6. Shared Ownership for Common Wealth.

Communities of interest work best when there is psychological ownership, financial interest, and transparency of governance. Organizations create psychological ownership through participation: they create financial interest through stock ownership programs; and they create transparency of governance through open-book management. If capitalism is to survive the twenty-first century it must develop a human face.[3] It must correct the growing inequities between rich and poor, and the haves and have nots. The biggest global issue in the twenty-first century will not be the creation of wealth but the sharing of wealth. As business consolidates its position as the most powerful institution on the planet, the pressures for distributing its wealth will increase. Sharing will become *the* most important global strategy for success.

Principle 7. Connectivity Builds Strength.

In times of fierce competition, the most successful organizations are always those that have the strongest alliances. Connectivity builds strength through shared ownership and risk. Both internal and external connectivity are necessary for the rapid flow of information and ideas. Structures and philosophies that block knowledge sharing are destined for extinction. Removing obstacles to the sharing of knowledge and the flow of ideas will occur only when organizations learn to build cultures that forsake self-interest for the common good.

Notes

1. Ann Svendsen, *The Stakeholder Strategy: Profiting from Collaborative Business Relationships* (San Francisco: Berrett-Koehler, 1998).

2. Daniel S. Hanson, *Cultivating Common Ground: Releasing the Power of Relationships at Work* (Boston: Butterworth-Heinemann, 1997).

3. Jeff Gates, *The Ownership Solution: Toward a Shared Capitalism for the 21ˢᵗ Century* (Reading, MA: Addison Wesley Longman, 1998).

Index

Butterworth-Heinemann Business Books . . . for Transforming Business

5th Generation Management, Co-creating Through Virtual Enterprising, Dynamic Teaming, and Knowledge Networking, Revised Edition,
Charles M. Savage, 0-7506-9701-6

Beyond Strategic Vision: Effective Corporate Action with Hoshin Planning,
Michael Cowley and Ellen Domb, 0-7506-9843-8

Beyond Time Management: Business with Purpose,
Robert A. Wright, 0-7506-9799-7

The Breakdown of Hierarchy: Communicating in the Evolving Workplace,
Eugene Marlow and Patricia O'Connor Wilson, 0-7056-9746-6

Business and the Feminine Principle: The Untapped Resource,
Carol R. Frenier, 0-7506-9829-2

Cultivating Common Ground: Releasing the Power of Relationships at Work,
Daniel S. Hanson, 0-7506-9832-2

Flight of the Phoenix: Soaring to Success in the 21st Century,
John Whiteside and Sandra Egli, 0-7506-9798-9

Getting a Grip on Tomorrow: Your Guide to Survival and Success in the Changed World of Work,
Mike Johnson, 0-7506-9758-X

Innovation Strategy for the Knowledge Economy: The Ken *Awakening,*
Debra M. Amidon, 0-7506-9841-1

The Intelligence Advantage: Organizing for Complexity,
Michael D. McMaster, 0-7506-9792-X

The Knowledge Evolution: Expanding Organizational Intelligence,
Verna Allee, 0-7506-9842-X

Leadership in a Challenging World: A Sacred Journey,
Barbara Shipka, 0-7506-9750-4

Leading from the Heart: Choosing Courage over Fear in the Workplace,
Kay Gilley, 0-7506-9835-7

Learning to Read the Signs: Reclaiming Pragmatism in Business,
F. Byron Nahser, 0-7506-9901-9

Marketing Plans that Work: Targeting Growth and Profitability,
Malcolm H.B. McDonald and Warren J. Keegan, 0-7506-9828-4

A Place to Shine: Emerging from the Shadows at Work,
Daniel S. Hanson, 0-7506-9738-5

Power Partnering: A Strategy for Business Excellence in the 21st Century
Sean Gadman, 0-7506-9809-8

Resources for the Knowledge-Based Economy Series

> *Knowledge Management and Organizational Design,*
> Paul S. Myers, 0-7506-9749-0
>
> *Knowledge Management Tools,*
> Rudy L. Ruggles, III, 0-7506-9849-7
>
> *Knowledge in Organizations,*
> Laurence Prusak, 0-7506-9718-0
>
> *The Strategic Management of Intellectual Capital,*
> David A. Klein, 0-7506-9850-0

Setting the PACE® in Product Development: A Guide to Product And Cycle-time Excellence,
Michael E. McGrath, 0-7506-9789-X

Time to Take Control: The Impact of Change on Corporate Computer Systems,
Tony Johnson, 0-7506-9863-2

The Transformation of Management,
Mike Davidson, 0-7506-9814-4

Who We Could Be at Work, Revised Edition,
Margaret A. Lulic, 0-7506-9739-3

To purchase a copy of any Butterworth-Heinemann Business title, please visit your local bookstore or call 1-800-366-2665.

About the Author

Richard Barrett is a Fellow of the World Business Academy and former Values Coordinator at the World Bank. He started the World Bank Spiritual Unfoldment Society in 1993 and organized the World Bank's first International Conference on Ethics, Spiritual Values, and Sustainable Development in 1995. He left the World Bank in June 1997 to set up Richard Barrett and Associates LLC, an international Leadership and Management Consulting firm.

Richard is an internationally acclaimed keynote speaker and author on personal and corporate transformation. His speaking topics include:

Building Cultural Capital and Human Resource Capacity through Values-Based Leadership

Creating a Visionary Organization

Values, Work, and Leadership in the 21st Century

Richard Barrett is known as an agent of change and an architect of global transformation. He supports leaders around the world in building cultural capital, strengthening human resource capacity, and developing values-based leadership. He has also developed a series of Corporate Transformation Tools^SM to assist in this process.

Richard Barrett's first book A *Guide to Liberating Your Soul* was published by Fulfilling Books in 1995. *Liberating the Corporate Soul* is his second book. Through his work and writings he is helping to shape the emerging business paradigms. Many of these writings and information on the Corporate Transformation Tools^SM can be accessed through his web site: http://www.corptools.com.

Richard Barrett can be contacted at 1 (800) 994-7986 or via e-mail at richard@corptools.com.